Wonder, Love and Praise

DATE DUE

Wonder, Love and Praise

A Companion to
The Methodist Worship Book

Neil Dixon

EPWORTH PRESS

British Library Cataloguing in Publication data

A catalogue record for this book is available
from the British Library

07162 0575 0

First published by Epworth Press
4 John Wesley Road
Werrington
Peterborough PE4 6ZP

Printed and bound in Great Britain by
Biddles Ltd, www.biddles.co.uk

This book is dedicated
to my wife, Julie,
to our children, Thomas and Emily,
and to the members of
the Liturgical Sub-Committee
of the Methodist Church.

Contents

Author's Note

It was not until November 1999 that the Faith and Order Committee decided that the new service book should be called *The Methodist Worship Book*. The Liturgical Sub-Committee had proposed the title *Wonder, Love and Praise*, though some of its members preferred *In Wonder, Love and Praise*, but the Faith and Order Committee felt that a self-explanatory name was needed. That decision has left the more imaginative title available for use in the present book.

Preface

A few months after the publication of *The Methodist Service Book* (1975), I was asked to write a short commentary on it (*At Your Service*, 1976). A quarter of a century later, I received a request to do something similar for the successor to the 1975 book, *The Methodist Worship Book* (1999). In 1975, I was to some extent handicapped by the fact that I had not been involved in any way in the preparation of the liturgical texts about which I was writing; I had been a student of liturgy for some years and had published a short book about worship, geared to a Methodist readership, but those, such as they were, were my only qualifications for writing the commentary. By contrast, first as Convener and then as Secretary of the Faith and Order Committee and as Convener, Chair and Secretary of its Liturgical Sub-Committee, I was heavily involved in the preparation of *The Methodist Worship Book* from start to finish. In 1975, it was easier for me to write dispassionately and objectively, though I had to ask many questions of those who had drafted *The Methodist Service Book* before I could produce my commentary. This time round, I have a greater sense of personal involvement with my subject!

While the work was in progress and after its completion, I wrote several articles and delivered a number of public lectures about it, and those who have read the former or heard the latter may recognize some ideas and maybe some actual sentences in the present book. For the most part, however, I have tried not to reproduce what has previously appeared in print. But I am grateful to the Methodist Sacramental Fellowship for permission to use a substantial part of my lecture, 'At your Service – Again!'

In the pages which follow, I offer an account of the reasons for the production of *The Methodist Worship Book* and the processes by which it came into being. Then comes a discussion of some of the significant issues (such as our understanding of God and our use of language) which had to be addressed during the book's preparation. A commentary on each section of *The Methodist Worship Book* follows. I have added a Glossary, recognizing that what I have written may be read by some people with little knowledge of liturgical terms or by those who are not familiar with distinctively Methodist terminology.

If footnotes and detailed references to other books had been included, this commentary would have been very much longer. I did not think that most readers would welcome that, and so I have kept such references to a minimum. I am of course indebted to many other publications, particularly for information about the sources of various texts.

In writing about the individual items in services, I have cited in brackets the numbers that appear against them in *The Methodist Worship Book*. And unless the context suggests otherwise, all page numbers in brackets refer to *The Methodist Worship Book*.

The opening paragraphs of the Acknowledgements (p. 601) address the possibility that some 'borrowed' material in *The Methodist Worship Book* may have been so radically amended that its original source can no longer be detected. Although great care was taken to identify sources, it was perhaps inevitable that some would be overlooked. In the period that has elapsed since the book's publication, and especially in the preparation of the present work, I have sought to trace sources that had not been acknowledged. The information given here, therefore, supplements and occasionally corrects the Acknowledgements in *The Methodist Worship Book*.

I am very grateful to members of the Liturgical Sub-Committee for their colleagueship over many years and for the help that they have given me in the tracing of sources and in providing other information. My adult children, Thomas and Emily, have spent many hours in reading various drafts of this book and have made innumerable helpful suggestions for its improvement in terms of accuracy, clarity and style. I take this opportunity to thank them for that; and to record my indebtedness to them, and to my wife, Julie, for the love, support and forbearance with which they have coped with me over the years.

I regard myself as extremely privileged to have been involved in the preparation of *The Methodist Worship Book*. My colleagues on the Faith and Order Committee, and especially the Liturgical Sub-Committee, brought to the task a great deal of experience, expertise, commitment and flair. The wider Methodist public, through the consultation exercise which I have described in Chapter One, helped to refine the draft services which they had the opportunity to study and use. Methodist and ecumenical consultants made shrewd and helpful observations. To have been part of this exercise, which involved consultation and collaboration at every stage, was a great joy to me.

The Methodist Church now has the largest and richest authorized liturgical text (apart from hymn books) that has ever been available to it. It is my hope that this commentary will encourage those who use the book, in whatever capacity, to appreciate its contents and to use them well, to the glory of God.

Neil Dixon

Introduction

Methodists, like many other Christians, are ambivalent about changes in worship. On the one hand, there are people who are always looking for something new. On the other, there are those who are instinctively resistant to change, especially when an authorized hymn book or service book is about to be replaced. The latter attitude was evident in 1983 when *Hymns & Psalms* was authorized as the successor to *The Methodist Hymn Book*, which by then was 50 years old. Since *The Methodist Worship Book* was 'authorized by the Methodist Conference for use in the Methodist Church' when its predecessor had been in use for a mere 23 years, some justification may be needed.

The Methodist Service Book, published in 1975 after several years of preparation and experimentation, had an immense impact on British Methodism. It brought many of the insights of the Liturgical Movement into the weekly worship of country chapels and suburban churches. It assisted the decline of the 'afterthought' communion (parts of the service of Holy Communion, added on to the end of a full-length preaching service); indeed it not only encouraged the use of the full service of word and sacrament, but also promoted more frequent celebrations of Holy Communion. *The Methodist Service Book* also brought about an increased use of the lectionary, since the ecumenical lectionary printed in it was far more 'user friendly' than the one previously offered. In general, *The Methodist Service Book* introduced British Methodism to what was then contemporary liturgical English, a more truly 'modern' form of language than that which had been provided by *The Book of Offices* (1936), and to services that were clearly and effectively structured, with joy and thanksgiving at their centre. By supplying advice about non-eucharistic Sunday worship, *The Methodist Service Book* also discouraged the sort of 'preaching service' where everything led up to the sermon and nothing much followed. All these developments, though none of them was without its critics, did much to enhance Methodist worship.

By 1990, however, it was clear that *The Methodist Service Book*, which had been published 15 years previously, was ripe for substantial revision or complete replacement. As one of the earliest authorized denominational service books of its vintage, it had preceded the Church of England's and the United Reformed Church's books by five years. It was, therefore, a trail-blazer, but inevitably developments occurred after its publication that would have had an impact upon it if it had been published later. Not many years after 1975, for instance, some important new ecumenical versions of 'common texts', like the Creeds, appeared, with the result that the *Methodist Service Book* versions seemed somewhat out of date.

Concern about inclusive language was not as widespread in the early 1970s as it is today, and as it had already become by 1990 (though it is only fair to add that the 1974 Conference rejected an impassioned appeal for the removal of sexist terms from the proposed services, sensitivity in this area being then confined to relatively few representatives). But, as the present writer insisted in the *Epworth Review* (September 1990):

> It would be unthinkable today to present to the Conference a service that included the words, '. . . that they may seek justice and peace for all men', yet those words appear on page B7 of *The Methodist Service Book*.

The issue of inclusive language, important in itself, was also indicative of a greater and more general reality: the Methodist Church of 1990 was not the Methodist Church of 1975. In all manner of ways the Church had moved on. This can be illustrated by reference to 'The Sunday Service', the complete order for word and sacrament which was probably the most influential feature of *The Methodist Service Book*. Anyone who had ever looked at a modern Anglican or Roman Catholic service book was aware that four eucharistic prayers (versions of what *The Methodist Service Book* called 'The Great Prayer of Thanksgiving') were supplied. There was inbuilt variety within the eucharistic liturgy. This prompted many Methodists to ask why they had only one Great Prayer, when others had four. The answer was not hard to discover. In the Methodism of 1975, when the Lord's Supper was celebrated relatively infrequently, it seemed to the Faith and Order Committee necessary to introduce a form of modern-language Communion Service that would become normative; such a service needed to be as accessible as possible, with some provision for variety, certainly, but with as much material as possible that would rapidly become familiar. Thus, one Great Prayer was enough, since many congregations would encounter it no more than once a month.

By 1990, when the proposals for a new service book came to the Conference, 'The Sunday Service' had become the victim of its own success. In many places the Lord's Supper was being celebrated more frequently than in 1975, to such an extent that some of the texts, such as the Great Prayer, had become more than familiar, even, some said, tedious. More variety was probably neither necessary nor even desirable in 1975. By 1990 it was greatly desired.

British Methodism also experienced, after 1975, a growing awareness of the Charismatic Movement and of the vitality of black-led churches. There was increasing exposure to styles of worship very different from old-fashioned 'preaching services' and very different, too, from 'formal' liturgies. Opinions varied greatly about the impact such considerations could or should have on the content of a service book, but it was clear that many expectations of worship in 1990 differed significantly from those current when *The Methodist Service Book* was published.

After the authorization of *The Methodist Service Book* in 1975, successive Conveners of the Faith and Order Committee carefully filed correspondence related to the book. The number of letters increased as time went on: there were criticisms of whole services, or details within them; suggestions for improvements; pleas for other forms of service to be provided. It was becoming clear, for example, that there was a widespread desire for more liturgical material for use before and after funerals, that resource material for 'preaching services' would be welcomed, and that there was a range of occasions for which liturgical provision had not previously been made where its absence was regretted. All these considerations pointed to the need for a new and more comprehensive book.

I

The Making of *The Methodist Worship Book*

The Faith and Order Committee's report to the Methodist Conference in 1990 included a recommendation that the Conference should authorize the Committee to start work on a successor to *The Methodist Service Book*. The adoption of that resolution triggered a process which culminated in the publication of *The Methodist Worship Book* almost nine years later.

According to Standing Order 330(9), the Faith and Order Committee

> is authorised to make proposals to the Conference for the revision from time to time of the forms of service authorised by the Conference for use in the Methodist Church, and forms of worship intended for regular and general use in the Methodist Church shall be submitted to the Conference after a period of experimentation on the recommendation of the committee.

The Faith and Order Committee was thus the obvious and proper body to be entrusted with the task of preparing the proposed new book. But the Committee had many other tasks to fulfil. Several major reports and a new Conference Statement were prepared while work on *The Methodist Worship Book* was proceeding. The Committee had recognized from the outset that, although it carried ultimate responsibility for the new book, subject to the Conference, the detailed drafting of services would need to be done by a sub-committee. So the Liturgical Sub-Committee was appointed, a group of 15 people who met in plenary session 30 times, mainly residentially, over a total of

70 days, between November 1990 and June 1998. Most of the meetings took place either at the Cherwell Centre, Oxford, or Whaley Hall, Derbyshire, though several other conference centres and retreat houses accommodated the Liturgical Sub-Committee on various occasions, and four annual five-day meetings were held at Knuston Hall, near Wellingborough.

In November 1990, in Oxford, members of the Liturgical Sub-Committee held their first meeting, joined on this occasion by two representatives of the Faith and Order Committee and by the Reverend A. Raymond George, who had been the principal architect of *The Methodist Service Book*, and who served as a consultant throughout the following years. At this first meeting, a proposed list of contents for the new book was discussed and agreed. Although this list was modified and rearranged many times during succeeding years, its adoption allowed the Sub-Committee to draw up a plan of action.

It was agreed that, as well as meeting in plenary session several times each year, the Liturgical Sub-Committee would be divided into three groups. The task of drafting particular sections of the book would be allocated to each group. A few modifications to this plan of action were made over the next few years, as some groups were able to make more rapid progress than others, but such changes were relatively minor. In the end, the allocation of responsibility turned out to be as follows:

Group One produced the first drafts of:

> Entry into the Church
> Holy Communion
> Marriage and the Blessing of a Marriage
> Admission, Commissioning and Welcome Services
> Pastoral Services.

Group Two did the initial work on:

> Morning, Afternoon and Evening Services
> Healing and Reconciliation Services
> Funeral and Related Services
> Calendar, Collects and Lectionary.

The first drafts of the following services were the responsibility of Group Three:

Daily Prayer
Holy Week Services
The Covenant Service
Ordination Services.

After the Oxford meeting, therefore, the three groups started to meet separately between plenary meetings of the Liturgical Sub-Committee. Each group had its own method of working, but a common feature was the tendency to allocate the production of first drafts to individual members of a group.

This can be illustrated by reference to Group One's work on Holy Communion. At a very early stage, it was agreed by the group (and subsequently by the Liturgical Sub-Committee and the Faith and Order Committee) that there should be several services of Holy Communion. (The reasons for this will be discussed in Chapter Eight.) It would have been difficult, if not impossible, for the members of Group One to meet together with blank sheets of paper and to produce all these services. So individual members of the group were asked to produce first drafts. One person did the initial work on 'Holy Communion for Advent'; another member was entrusted with the first draft of 'Holy Communion for Christmas and Epiphany'; a third undertook to draft 'Holy Communion for Lent and Passiontide'; and so on. Over a period of a few months, first drafts were available of several services. Group One worked through these drafts at its meetings, rewriting and refining them all. So each member of Group One contributed to the services of Holy Communion both by producing one first draft (or more than one, in the case of some members) and by helping to revise the drafts prepared by other members of the Group.

It is worth observing that those who engage in liturgical work in committees need thick skins! Seeing someone's blue pencil striking through one's purple passages is not easy. Drafters must not be too proprietorial or defensive. What one individual has written can almost always be improved when several people give detailed attention to it.

When Group One had, for the time being, completed its work on the Communion Services, texts were circulated to all members of the Liturgical Sub-Committee, who discussed them in plenary session. Not surprisingly, members of Groups Two and Three could think of improvements to suggest, and further revision took place before the texts of these services were submitted to the Faith and Order Committee.

Meanwhile, a similar process was taking place in the other groups, who presented their work to the Liturgical Sub-Committee as soon as they were able. After making further revisions, the Liturgical Sub-Committee reported to the Faith and Order Committee.

The task given to the Faith and Order Committee in 1990 was to bring proposals to the Conference, in due course, for a successor to *The Methodist Service Book*. It would have been possible, therefore, for the Committee to revise and approve the services prepared for it by the Liturgical Sub-Committee, to stockpile them, and to present them *en masse* to the Conference when all were ready. But this would have been unwise. It seemed to the Committee vital that the Methodist people should be as fully involved as possible in the process of preparing the new book. So in 1991, the Committee's report to the Conference included these words:

> The Faith and Order Committee believes that it is of the utmost importance that the widest possible trial of new material, and consultation about it, should take place before the Conference is asked to authorize it. The Committee therefore requests the Conference to permit it to publish draft services, not seen or authorized by the Conference, in a form which can readily be copied and used by local churches, so as to allow experiment and wide consultation to take place in an effective and inexpensive way before any new material is presented for the Conference's authorization.

The Conference authorized this procedure and thus set in motion a remarkable process of trial and consultation. From 1992 onwards, draft orders of service were issued by the Faith and Order Committee, with permission for the drafts to be copied for local use. Nearly 25,000 'originals' were purchased and the photocopiers of Methodism started to grow hot. About 1,500 letters, many of them long and containing detailed comments, were received by the Committee.

Every comment was listed and carefully considered by the Liturgical Sub-Committee, and all the services which had been issued for trial use were substantially revised in the light of these comments. That is not to say that it was possible, or would even have been desirable, for the Liturgical Sub-Committee to respond positively to every single suggestion. The same text proved capable of arousing very different comments, such as, 'We were greatly moved by this lovely prayer' and 'Please do not include this dreadful prayer.' Some suggestions were so eccentric that it would have been impossible to include them in what was to be an authorized worship book. But the consultation exercise was enormously successful. It caused the Liturgical Sub-Committee to reassess its texts, drawing on experience of their use (a crucial matter, for liturgy is much more than words on a page), and to wrestle with the theological and stylistic criticisms contained among the comments. It also enabled British Methodists to feel, correctly, that their voices had been heard, with the result that the number of amendments to the 'final' text proposed at the 1998 Conference was relatively small. The Liturgical Sub-Committee was assisted in its work, not only by the comments received in this way, but also by the advice of consultants, both Methodist and from other churches, both from Britain and from other parts of the world.

Some significant changes which the consultation process brought about are noted in the following chapters, but it is worth observing, at this stage, a few general issues which emerged during the period of consultation. First, there was a resounding affirmation of what correspondents had previously written to the Faith and Order Committee to say: there was clearly a widespread desire for substantial liturgical provision. *The Methodist Worship Book* is a large book because that is what the Methodist people asked for – not in so many words, of course, but by requesting, for instance, the provision of much more material for funerals, more variety in Communion Services, the inclusion of healing and commissioning services, and so forth.

Second, the consultation process made it clear that British Methodism was now far more aware of, and indeed appreciative of, the changing seasons of the Christian year than had once been the case. The provision of seasonal material in the early draft services was widely welcomed.

Third, the issue of language (which is addressed at some length in Chapter Three) was one about which some correspondents felt strongly. On the one hand, there was concern that the language employed in new services should be intelligible, and the view was expressed that some of the earlier draft services were unnecessarily long and unduly wordy. This was a fair comment, of which the Liturgical Sub-Committee took due notice. On the other hand, there was firm support for the idea that liturgical language should be beautiful and 'uplifting'.

The task of further revision was undertaken in a number of different ways. The earliest texts to be made available for use, the services of Holy Communion, attracted by far the most comments. The Liturgical Sub-Committee invited three people, none of whom was a member of the Sub-Committee nor, at that time, of the Faith and Order Committee, to consider the draft Communion Services and all the comments on them, and to make recommendations. This independent evaluation resulted in a report which extended to 111 pages, and which enabled Group One and subsequently the Liturgical Sub-Committee greatly to improve the services.

Some of the shorter services were refined, in response to the comments received, in plenary meetings of the Liturgical Sub-Committee, and yet other services were redrafted first by the appropriate group, then by the Liturgical Sub-Committee.

In the early stages of the work, the Faith and Order Committee itself adopted a policy of allowing services which it had received from the Liturgical Sub-Committee to be issued for trial use without spending a great deal of time in further revising them. This was a sensible policy, because it was clear that substantial revision was likely to result from the consultation exercise, though, equally clearly, many members of the Faith and Order Committee found it difficult to refrain from making suggestions for improvement.

At a later stage, from 1995 onwards, it was necessary for the Committee to devote many hours to the texts of the services. The Committee, after all, was the body whose responsibility it was to present the proposed text of the new book to the Conference, and its members did not treat this responsibility lightly. At one meeting, when about half a dozen services were presented for final approval, members were asked to send in proposed amendments in advance of the meeting. Almost 200 proposed amendments were received, each of which had to be considered by the Committee.

The 1990 report which instigated the whole process had indicated that the work could not be completed in less than five years. In fact, it became clear within a couple of years that it was unlikely that a final text could be presented to the Conference before 1997 or 1998. By 1996 it was obvious that the later date would apply, and consideration began to be given to how the Conference could best be helped to consider and, it was hoped, authorize for use what was going to be a substantial book. The prospect of nearly 400 representatives wanting to engage in liturgical revision was daunting. There were clear memories of the Reverend A. Raymond George, as the Convener of the Faith and Order Committee, presenting the services that would form *The Methodist Service Book* to the Conference of 1974 and responding to amendments as they were proposed, without notice, from the floor of the Conference. Such events could not happen in 1998, because amendments had to be tabled in advance, as notices of motion, and printed on the Conference's Order Paper. Nevertheless, it would be very difficult for the Conference to deal with a large number of amendments.

The Conference of 1997 therefore adopted procedures to be

followed in 1998. A draft edition of *The Methodist Worship Book* would be sent to every member of the Conference in March 1998. All proposed amendments, with the names of their proposers and seconders, would be required to be received by the Conference Office in early June. Between the Ministerial and Representative Sessions of the Conference, a Revision Committee (constituted in accordance with Standing Orders) would meet to consider each proposed amendment. The printed report of the Revision Committee's recommendations would be in the hands of every Conference representative in time for proposed amendments to those recommendations to be notified on the Order Paper. Apart from recommendations that had attracted proposed amendments, the Conference would vote on the Revision Committee's recommendations without debate.

In the event, fewer proposals for amendments were received from members of the Conference than had been thought likely, though quite enough (nearly 70) to justify the procedures that were in place. The Liturgical Sub-Committee met a week or so before the Revision Committee to guide the Faith and Order Committee's two representatives (who were to have speaking but not voting rights at the Revision Committee meeting) as to how to respond to the various proposals. There were several which the Liturgical Sub-Committee was happy to accept; others which it could accept in principle, but would want to modify; and a few which it felt should be strongly resisted.

The Revision Committee met in two sessions for a total of seven hours, treating every proposed amendment with the utmost seriousness, and carefully weighing every argument put forward by proposers and seconders, by the Faith and Order Committee representatives and by its own members. The Committee's report was duly published and only six or seven of its recommendations were challenged. It is worth noting that one of these concerned the controversial words, 'God, our Father and our Mother'.

In 1992, one of the draft services of Holy Communion, issued for trial use and comment, addressed God as 'our Father and our Mother'. Hardly anything else in the draft services attracted so much adverse comment (though no more than 40 people in all commented on this expression, of whom about one-fifth were in favour of it). It seemed to the Faith and Order Committee that it could not retain these words when so many correspondents were opposed to them.

Though the words 'and our Mother' were therefore absent from the draft edition supplied to Conference members, the Revision Committee recommended the adoption of a proposal that they be included in the Great Prayer of Thanksgiving in 'Holy Communion during Ordinary Seasons (Second Service)'. The attempt to overturn the Revision Committee's recommendation was unsuccessful, the Conference voting by a substantial majority to insert the words in the recommended place.

This rather extreme example illustrates the process of consultation and revision which preceded the authorization of *The Methodist Worship Book*. Several stages of drafting, reconsideration, revision and further reconsideration are discernible:

1 The words 'God, our Father and our Mother' are included in a draft service.
2 The words 'and our Mother' attract a mixed, though largely adverse, reaction.
3 These words are omitted from the draft edition submitted to the Conference.
4 An amendment is proposed that the words be inserted in one service.
5 The Revision Committee recommends that the amendment be accepted.
6 The Revision Committee's recommendation is challenged in the Conference.
7 The Conference upholds the recommendation.

The process of writing services, receiving and reacting to comments, and revising services, and the passage of the completed text through the Revision Committee and the Conference are, of course, only parts of the story. *The Methodist Worship Book* would not have seen the light of day without the wholeheartedly enthusiastic and imaginative involvement of the Methodist Publishing House, whose staff worked long hours in getting various editions ready. The draft edition, for example, had to be set, printed, bound and dispatched between December 1997, when the Faith and Order Committee approved the final texts, and March 1998, when members of the Conference were due to receive their copies. It was a cause of great gratification when advance orders for the Conference-authorized text far exceeded the expectations of either the Faith and Order Committee or the Methodist Publishing House.

It has never been the practice, in Methodist service books, to name those who have contributed to them, and, in truth, it would be impossible to name all those who, over a period of eight years, contributed in one way or another to *The Methodist Worship Book*. The membership of the Faith and Order Committee changed almost completely during that time, so that hardly anyone who was present when texts were considered by the Committee for the last time in 1997 had been involved when the project started in 1990. But the Liturgical Sub-Committee remained virtually unchanged throughout this time, and it is perhaps not inappropriate to end this account of the making of *The Methodist Worship Book* by listing its members. They were:

The Reverend Doctor Martyn D. Atkins
The Reverend Doctor Stuart J. Burgess
The Reverend Doctor Kenneth C. Carveley
Mr Dudley Coates
The Reverend Judy Davies
The Reverend Neil Dixon (Convener)
The Reverend John S. Lampard
The Reverend Donald Ker (representing the Irish Conference)
The Reverend Arthur Nelson
The Reverend Donald Pickard
Mrs Kathryn Schofield
Mrs Christine Sheasby (Christine Odell)
The Reverend Neil A. Stubbens (from 1994)
The Reverend Michael J. Townsend

The Reverend Doctor David H. Tripp (to 1992)
The Reverend C. Norman R. Wallwork.

Stuart Burgess, Neil Dixon, David Tripp and Norman Wallwork
had been members of the previous Liturgical Sub-Committee,
and Arthur Nelson had been involved in the preparation of *The
Methodist Service Book*.

At a relatively early stage in the Liturgical Sub-Committee's
work, it was decided that, for the use of Methodist churches in
Wales, a bilingual (Welsh/English) edition of *The Methodist
Worship Book* should be available and should be sold at the
same price as the English-only version. Succeeding draft services
were translated into Welsh. Clearly, every change made to the
English text required corresponding changes to the Welsh version, and changes continued to be made up to the Conference of
1998 (and indeed beyond, because the Conference empowered
its Secretary and the Secretary of the Faith and Order Committee
to correct any errors or inconsistencies that were discovered). At
a very late stage, however, it was discovered that, unknown to
the Methodist Publishing House and the Faith and Order
Committee, several services had not been translated into Welsh
at any time. Once again, the Methodist Publishing House rose to
the occasion magnificently. Translations were urgently commissioned and the Reverend Marian Jones, who had been a member
of the Faith and Order Committee, rendered invaluable service
against a very tight deadline by overseeing the typesetting and
layout of the Welsh text. It is a tribute to the dedication of all
involved that the bilingual version saw the light of day only a few
weeks after the publication of the English-only book.

2

The God whom we Worship

The publication of *The Methodist Worship Book* was marked by an extraordinary amount of media attention. Never before has the Methodist Church been given quite such extensive coverage by *GMTV*, ITV's *Sunday Morning*, Radio Four news, Radio Five Live, the BBC World Service, innumerable local radio stations, almost every national daily newspaper, some weekly publications, and scores of regional and local newspapers, not to mention the appearance on the *Vanessa* show of the Reverend Norman Wallwork, a member of the Liturgical Sub-Committee. The reason for all this media interest was one word, the word 'Mother' addressed to God in one eucharistic prayer, where the text reads, 'God our Father and our Mother, we give you thanks and praise.' There has been some discussion in Chapter One of the way in which the words 'and our Mother' came to be inserted in the prayer; we now consider their significance.

At one level, it is difficult to understand the attention that was paid to this single use of the words 'God . . . our Mother'. God is, after all, addressed or described as 'Father' over 400 times in *The Methodist Worship Book*, and as 'Mother' only once. But some critics of the address argued that one occurrence is one too many.

The language used by a service book to speak of or to God clearly reflects a major issue for the writers and users of liturgical texts: what sort of God do we believe in and seek to worship?

From the time of its publication in 1975 onwards, *The Methodist Service Book* was criticized by some people on the grounds that it presented an image of God in which concepts like omnipotence and lordship predominated. Masculine power images, it was said, occurred altogether too frequently in prayers

('Almighty God', 'King of the universe', 'Lord'). The collects were cited particularly in this respect. But this was not simply a question of masculine terms: the book, the critics suggested, like many other liturgical sources, did not adequately portray God as fundamentally loving, fundamentally gracious, fundamentally self-emptying. There was far too much about power and king-ship, glory and lordship. There was far too little that reflected the suffering, self-giving God revealed in Jesus.

In 1989 the Faith and Order Committee set up a Working Party to look at the specific question of the language and imagery that the Church uses about God, 'in the context of our concern for inclusivity and our understanding of male and female created in God's image', to quote the Working Party's terms of reference. The resultant report, *Inclusive Language and Imagery about God*, was approved by the Faith and Order Committee and adopted by the Methodist Conference in 1992. The report argued that the Bible itself uses considerably more images than is generally recognized and it encouraged the exploration of a wider range of imagery in speaking to or about God.

The Liturgical Sub-Committee treated this issue with the utmost seriousness. While resisting calls from some quarters for an abandonment of traditional Trinitarian language and of 'masculine' or 'power' words like 'Almighty', 'Father', 'Lord', and 'King', those who drafted the services made a determined effort to include other words and images which do justice to the Christian understanding of God as loving, gracious, self-emptying and self-giving. The 'Collects' well illustrate this point. The Liturgical Sub-Committee was conscious that this section of the book provided an especially promising place at which to supplement the traditional forms of address ('Almighty God', 'Everlasting God') with other forms. Of the seven collects printed on pp. 536 and 537, for example, one begins 'Almighty God' and another 'God our Father', which are traditional 'power' terms or 'masculine' images. The other five begin 'O God, rich in mercy', 'God of compassion', 'Most merciful God', 'Eternal God', and 'God of all-redeeming grace'. The traditional biblical imagery, including 'power' language, has not been expunged from the book. But alongside it there is other imagery, which is equally biblical, imagery which recognizes and expresses the Church's belief in a God of compassion, grace, mercy and love. This provision can only enrich our liturgical expression of our understanding of God.

The controversy, such as it was, about the address, 'God our Father and our Mother', raises an important question about imagery. As the 1992 report made clear, the Bible uses a wide range of images to describe or refer to God. Most of these images are masculine, admittedly, but among them there certainly are some feminine ones. Deuteronomy 32.18, Psalm 22.9, Psalm 131.2, Isaiah 42.14 and Isaiah 66.13 are examples. They have influenced our hymnody ('as with a mother's tender hand . . .'; 'he like a mother doth speed'). Sometimes, the Bible uses inanimate objects or forces as images for God – fire, for instance, or rock. It is not self-evident that it is acceptable to address Christ as 'Rock of ages' and the Holy Spirit as 'refining fire', but not acceptable to follow the example of Scripture by using female, as well as male and neutral, imagery for God.

The argument has been advanced that, while it may be permissible to say that God is, in some respects, **like** a mother, it is wrong to **address** God as 'Mother'. This argument draws too sharp a distinction between simile and metaphor. In everyday conversation, human beings are well able to understand the role of metaphor. A person does not think that someone who calls her 'pet' has mistaken her for a cat or a hamster. If we pause to reflect, we know perfectly well that when we call Jesus a 'rock' we are using an image. The same is true when we call God 'Father', as we must certainly continue to do. For 'Father', though a perfectly proper – indeed normative – word to use when speaking to God, is just as much an example of imagery as 'mother', 'shepherd' or 'rock'.

The God in whom we believe is neither male nor female. God is beyond gender. God is spirit. All words are inadequate to describe or address God. But we need to use words, and some of the best available words come from the language of human relationships. If, as Genesis insists, human beings, both male and female, were created in God's image, then, however incompletely and faintly, both male and female images can help us to express our understanding of God. In the Lord's Prayer, Jesus taught his disciples to call God 'Father', but he never suggested that they should use no other prayer or form of address. Nor has the Church used only that one image, precious and fundamental though it is. Hymnody has perhaps been ahead of other liturgical forms in using a wide range of images. 'Captain of Israel's host', 'a sea without a shore', 'Lord of creation', 'my soul's shelter', 'a safe stronghold' are all examples of images, other than 'Father', which have been used to address the First Person of the Trinity.

If *The Methodist Worship Book* had abandoned the use of 'Father' in speaking to or about God, it would have turned its back on the teaching of Jesus and centuries of Christian tradition. But it has done nothing of the sort. 'Father' is still there, abundantly, and so too are words such as 'Lord' and 'King'. There are also scores of examples of 'gender neutral' addresses – 'God of all holiness', 'living God', 'God of beauty and light', for instance – as well as the one clearly female image, drawn from the Bible itself, which supplement traditional liturgical images.

The God whom we worship is far beyond words, beyond gender, beyond 'our scanty thought'. By employing a wide range of terms to describe and address God, however, *The Methodist Worship Book* enriches our understanding, enlarges our thoughts. The ancient saying, *Lex orandi, lex credendi* (literally, 'the rule of what is to be prayed is the rule of what is to be believed'), is a reminder of the intimate connection between doctrine and worship. What we say to and about the God whom we worship must reflect and express our theological understanding.

3

Language and Liturgy

The previous chapter was principally concerned with the understanding of God which undergirds *The Methodist Worship Book*. Inevitably, therefore, since a service book must express its understanding of God in words, some attention has already been given to the use of language in *The Methodist Worship Book*. But there are other issues about language and liturgy which need to be explored, and that is the purpose of this chapter.

Inclusive Language

The matter of inclusive language, though important, can be briefly addressed. In the Introduction it was pointed out that one of the charges levelled against *The Methodist Service Book* was its use of non-inclusive language to refer to human beings. In 1975, few people (though there were some) thought it offensive to pray 'for the salvation of mankind' or that we might use God's gifts 'to set men free from drudgery' or to confess 'that we have sinned against our fellow men'. The use of inclusive language is now more or less taken for granted among all but the most unreformed of Methodists, and it can be said with confidence that *The Methodist Worship Book* never uses the word 'men', when 'men, women and children' is the sense intended, or indeed any other form of exclusive language in reference to human beings.

Liturgical Language

What sort of language is appropriate for a worship book that is intended to last for several years? Part of the answer is implied by the question: the language needs to have durability, to bear frequent repetition. Not all liturgies need that sort of language. Some published prayers, for example, contain unusual and striking images, which, when first encountered, are remarkably moving aids to worship. When they are used for a second time, their effect is a little diminished. By the third or fourth occasion, the imagery begins to pall. This does not really matter much; there is certainly a place for imaginative liturgical language, ephemeral though it tends to be. But an authorized worship book must strive to provide texts that can be used again and again, perhaps surviving for a generation or more. Its language must, therefore, avoid the sort of images and expressions which are either strikingly unusual or simply banal.

Furthermore, the language of a worship book must be capable of helping worshippers to get beyond mere intellectual understanding. It should assist the creation of an appropriate atmosphere of awe and wonder in the presence of God. This is not to suggest that liturgical language should be obscure or incomprehensible. But in some ways, the atmosphere of an act of worship matters more than whether every worshipper understands every word. The 1993 Methodist Conference adopted a report which included the following comments:

> 'Simple English' is not easy to define. Certainly, the (Faith and Order) Committee is opposed to the introduction of unnecessarily complex words and phrases and constantly bears in mind, in preparing liturgies, the question of intelligibility. It is also the Committee's hope that material in the new book will reflect a range of styles. But Christian faith and devotion have a rich and splendid treasury of images from which to draw and we should not overlook the remarkable power of words to evoke an atmosphere of worship, even when not every word is

understood by everyone present. Among the many requests received by the Faith and Order Committee in connection with the new book, there have been several pleading for language which is beautiful, poetic and evocative. Such language need not be obscure, but it could not easily be described as simple.

Moreover, any organisation has its own 'peculiar' language. Lawyers or motor mechanics, talking to their peers, may well employ the English language in terms that are entirely understood among them, but which are difficult for others to understand. So it is with Christian people gathered together for worship. The rich, biblically-based theological heritage which informs our worship finds expression in liturgical language which to some extent needs to be learned by those who come to share in it. Such language at its best avoids unnecessary technicalities but may not always be 'simple' if simplicity is thought to consist in being immediately understandable to anyone encountering it for the first time. Even so, good liturgical language creates a sense of mystery (rather than merely mystification) and may help even those who do not understand every word to worship. An attempt to produce services in a style which is immediately accessible to everyone would run the risk of impoverishing worship by depriving it of a rich expression of the faith that underlies Christian worship.

It can indeed be argued that the language of prayer should be more akin to poetry than to prose. Most of the correspondents who commented on the style of the draft services during the consultation process were thrilled with the beauty of many of the prayers and other texts.

A good example is the lovely prayer which comes at the end of 'Prayer in the Morning' (p. 14):

Lord our God,
as with all creation
we offer you the life of this new day,
give us grace to love and serve you
to the praise of Jesus Christ our Lord.

Another is the glorious prayer at the end of 'Prayer in the Evening' (p. 24):

> Lord our God,
> at the ending of this day,
> and in the darkness and silence of this night,
> cover us with healing and forgiveness,
> that we may take our rest in peace;
> through Jesus Christ our Lord.

There is beauty in these evocative words from 'Holy Communion for Christmas and Epiphany' (p. 133):

> Searched for,
> Christ comes.
>
> To the wise and powerful,
> star-led to Bethlehem, seeking a king,
> he comes, child of Mary,
> crowned with meekness,
> worthy of every gift

and in these, from the same service (p. 136), which also appear at the Preparation of the Gifts (p. 191) in 'Holy Communion during Ordinary Seasons (First Service)':

> Lord and Giver of every good thing,
> we bring to you
> bread and wine for our communion,
> lives and gifts for your kingdom,
> all for transformation
> through your grace and love
> made known in Jesus Christ our Saviour.

The Great Prayer of Thanksgiving in 'Holy Communion for Advent' includes these words (p. 124):

God of all glory and light of our salvation,
we offer you thanks and praise
through Jesus Christ your Son our Lord.

By your living Word
you called all things into being,
breathed into life the desire of your heart
and shaped us in your own likeness.
Though we rejected your love,
you did not give us up
or cease to fashion our salvation.
You made a covenant to be our God,
spoke to us through the prophets,
and prepared the way for our redemption.

All these examples are of new material, specially written for
The Methodist Worship Book. Our next example of style and
imagery, however, is not new. It can be found in the Great Prayer
of Thanksgiving, leading into the *Sanctus* ('Holy, holy, holy Lord
. . .') in 'Holy Communion for the Easter Season' (p. 170):

Therefore with angels and archangels
and all the company of heaven
we bless and praise your glorious name, saying . . .

These venerable words were not to be found in 'The Sunday
Service' (1975), which offered at this point only the rather apolo-
getic

And so with the whole company of heaven we join in the
unending hymn of praise.

No 'angels and archangels' were deemed appropriate in a new
liturgy in 1975. But, compared with *The Methodist Hymn Book*
(1933) and *The Methodist Service Book*, *Hymns & Psalms*
(1983) and now *The Methodist Worship Book* demonstrate a
certain recovery of nerve. The compilers of *Hymns & Psalms*

were not afraid, for example, to restore many authentic texts, as in the treatment of 'When I survey the wondrous cross', where the vivid imagery of stanza four ('His dying crimson, like a robe, spreads o'er his body on the tree') was too much for the editors of *The Methodist Hymn Book*, even though that stanza is of pivotal importance to the text as a whole. And in *The Methodist Worship Book*, as we have seen, the 'angels and archangels', who were considered much too picturesque in 1975, have made a welcome return.

Another fascinating example of this recovery of nerve is the Prayer of Humble Access. For *The Methodist Service Book*, the prayer was completely rewritten as follows:

> Lord, we come to your table,
> trusting in your mercy
> and not in any goodness of our own.
> We are not worthy even to gather up the crumbs
>   under your table,
> but it is your nature always to have mercy,
> and on that we depend.
> So feed us with the body and blood
> of Jesus Christ, your Son,
> that we may for ever live in him
> and he in us.

But when the prayer appeared in a draft order in 1992, the text adopted in *The Alternative Service Book* (1980), which is very much closer to Thomas Cranmer's original, was used:

> We do not presume
> to come to this your table, merciful Lord,
> trusting in our own righteousness,
> but in your manifold and great mercies.
> We are not worthy
> so much as to gather up the crumbs
>   under your table.
> But you are the same Lord

whose nature is always to have mercy.
Grant us therefore, gracious Lord,
so to eat the flesh of your dear Son Jesus Christ
and to drink his blood,
that we may evermore dwell in him
and he in us.

The powerful Johannine imagery, retained in this version, has
survived into *The Methodist Worship Book* – another example
of our being less afraid than a generation ago of such evocative
language. But the consultation exercise also revealed that what
many people recognized as the Prayer of Humble Access was in
fact the 1975 version, and not the Cranmer text or something
more closely akin to it. In order to serve both those who rejoice
in the rich imagery of the original and those who have grown up
with the 1975 text, both versions were included in the five places
where the Prayer of Humble Access is printed.

Ecumenical Texts

Before we leave the matter of language, let us take a brief look at
the question of 'ecumenical texts'. Unlike some denominations,
which it would be discourteous to mention by name, the Methodist Church believed it to be right to use the current English
Language Liturgical Consultation translations, unaltered, for the
major common texts – *Agnus Dei*, 'Glory to God in the highest',
the Nicene Creed, the Apostles' Creed, *Sursum Corda, Sanctus,
Benedictus Qui Venit, Gloria Patri, Te Deum Laudamus, Benedictus, Magnificat, Nunc Dimittis* and the Lord's Prayer. The
English Language Liturgical Consultation is a body which represents the major churches in the English-speaking world; the
churches of Great Britain are represented on it through the Joint
Liturgical Group. The intention to use the Consultation's translations in *The Methodist Worship Book* without making any
alterations to them was not quite fulfilled; there are two texts
where the book has unintentionally deviated from the ecumenical

text. These will be noted in Chapter Five. Incidentally, the Consultation is incorrectly called a 'Commission' in the Acknowledgements (p. 602).

The Lord's Prayer is set out in two columns whenever it appears, the first containing the English Language Liturgical Consultation translation and the second the so-called 'modified traditional' version ('Our Father, who art in heaven . . .'). This is a notable development since 1975, when the International Consultation on English Texts versions, which at that time were widely acceptable, were all included in the body of the services, with the exception of the Lord's Prayer, which was relegated to an appendix. The practical effect of this was to ensure that the modern-language version was rarely used. What is done in *The Methodist Worship Book* makes it much easier for either the familiar or the modern-language version to be used. It will also be helpful to the growing number of people who do not know any version of the Lord's Prayer by heart.

4

Matters of General Relevance

Before we turn to an exploration of the services contained in *The Methodist Worship Book*, it may be helpful to consider a few further matters which are relevant to the book as a whole.

The Preface

The Preface to *The Methodist Worship Book* (pp. viif.) begins with a brief but important account of the theology of worship which informs the entire book before describing the book's pedigree and status. Although these two pages could easily be overlooked, much care was taken over their content and they deserve to be carefully read.

General Directions, Introductions and Notes

The Methodist Service Book of 1975 contained a large number of 'General Directions', which preceded each service or group of services and included instructions about what should happen during those services, quotations from Standing Orders or the Deed of Union, and other material, such as legal requirements in respect of marriages. A different system was adopted for *The Methodist Worship Book*.

First, it was decided that the term 'General Directions' should be used only for directions that were truly general, that is, those that applied to the whole book. There are six of these General Directions on p. ix. They deal with such matters as sensitivity to the needs of those who cannot respond to directions to stand or kneel, the use of hymns, and what should happen in respect of notices and collections.

Second, it was agreed that each service or group of services should have its own 'Introduction', which would provide appropriate – though brief – historical, theological and liturgical information. A good example is the Introduction to the 'Ordination Services' (pp. 297f.), which sets ordained ministry in the context of the ministry of the whole people of God, summarizes Methodism's historical development of presbyteral and diaconal ministry, and describes the Church's practice and understanding of ordination. The Introduction also provides important information about the tripartite nature of Methodist ordination prayers. These Introductions were included in order to help worshippers to take part in services with a good understanding of what those services are about.

Third, the services, or groups of services, are preceded, where necessary, by 'Notes'. It was decided that such Notes should be confined to purely liturgical directions, the sort of information or directions needed mainly by a person responsible for leading a service. The requirements of *The Constitutional Practice and Discipline of the Methodist Church* are not reproduced in the Notes, as they had been in some General Directions in *The Methodist Service Book*. It is interesting, in this regard, to compare the Notes to 'Confirmation and Reception into Membership' in *The Methodist Worship Book* with the General Directions to the equivalent service in *The Methodist Service Book*. Similarly, no information is given in the Notes to 'The Marriage Service' about any legal requirements (such as the need to give notice to a Superintendent Registrar) other than those which relate directly to the conduct of the service.

Some of the Notes may seem extremely detailed, even fussy; for example, the Notes which precede each of the services in the 'Entry into the Church' section of the book. But it was important to make it crystal clear which of the five services was appropriate in various different sets of circumstances and where it should occur within a total act of worship. Even if some Notes still seem

over-detailed, at least *The Methodist Worship Book* has avoided
the inclusion of anything approaching the extraordinary General
Direction in *Entry into the Church* (1991), which reads: 'When
Baptism is administered in a baptistry, river, lake, or the sea, the
pouring of water into a font is of course omitted.'

Rubrics

Rubrics are words, phrases or sentences within services which
give directions or information to those taking part. Examples
are: 'The people stand'; 'The elements that remain are covered
with a white cloth'; 'A seasonal introduction to the blessing may
be said.' *The Methodist Worship Book*, like its predecessor,
prints rubrics in their proper colour, red (the Latin word, *ruber*,
means 'red'). This clearly distinguishes them from words which
are meant to be spoken by the leader or the congregation.

Some rubrics are permissive, as, for example: 'A lighted candle
may be given to the *parents* or *godparents* of each child.' The
word 'may' makes it clear that this is a permissive rubric, which
allows for the possibility that a candle will be given, while also
allowing for the possibility that it will not. Other rubrics,
however, assume that what is rubricated for will actually occur:
'The minister makes the sign of the cross on the forehead of each
child . . .' Writers of liturgical texts need to take as much care
in the drafting of rubrics as in the provision of words to be
spoken.

Typographical Matters

As we have seen, rubrics are printed in red type; words to be
spoken are printed in black. Other typographical conventions in
The Methodist Worship Book are the use of **bold** type to denote
words spoken by the whole congregation and of *italic* letters, in
both spoken text and rubrics, where there may be need to adjust
the text or where the rubric envisages more than one set of

circumstances. Examples of these uses of italic script can be found on p. 64:

3 The *candidates* for Baptism who *are* able to answer for *themselves stand.*

  The minister says to *them*:

  N *and* N *(N)*, having heard these things . . .

Italics are used in these rubrics because it may be the case that there is only one candidate who is a person able to answer for herself or himself. If this is so, only that one person (N) will be addressed in the spoken text.

Quotations from the Bible

Many services include not only biblical references, but also Bible passages set out in full. After careful consideration, it was decided that the *New Revised Standard Version of the Bible (Anglicized Edition)* should be used for all such passages, unless there were compelling reasons to use another translation in a particular case. Though other translations had their advocates, the Faith and Order Committee believed that the *New Revised Standard Version* has three qualities which make it admirable for the purpose: it is an accurate translation; it is suitable for public reading; and it avoids 'exclusive' language wherever possible.

Bible Readings and Psalms

Many of the services in *The Methodist Worship Book* indicate that there should be two or three readings from Scripture. In the case of services of Holy Communion, where by long tradition there is invariably a Gospel reading, these readings would norm- ally be an Old Testament passage and/or an Epistle, as well as the Gospel. The rubrics on p. 121 and elsewhere make this clear. In some other services (see for example p. 31), there is scope for greater flexibility about the sources of the Bible readings.

Psalms, it will be noted, are mentioned separately in these rubrics. Psalms should not be thought of as Old Testament readings, but as hymns, ideally said or sung by the whole congregation, perhaps antiphonally. This reflects the practice of the early Church (Colossians 3.16), which itself continued the custom of worship in the synagogue. *The Methodist Worship Book* almost always treats Psalms as hymns, although there are a very few occasions (see, for instance, p. 507) where the book deviates from its normal course in this respect.

Declarations of Forgiveness, Blessings and Dismissals

Notice of Motion No. 19, concerning declarations of forgiveness, blessings and dismissals, appeared in the Methodist Conference Order Paper for 24 June 1996. It was withdrawn by its proposer and seconder after the Secretary of the Faith and Order Committee had given an assurance that the Committee would consider what it asked for, discuss the best way of meeting its concerns, and report to the Conference of 1997.

The Motion read:

> Conference directs the Faith and Order Committee to ensure that both second and first person forms are provided for all declarations of forgiveness, congregational blessings, benedictions and dismissals in the new *Methodist Service Book*.

The Faith and Order Committee reported to the 1997 Conference as follows:

> The suggestion is sometimes made that declarations of forgiveness, blessings, and so on, spoken in the second person form (for example, 'The blessing of God . . . remain with you always') distance the speaker from those addressed and may even suggest that the speaker does not believe that he or she

needs forgiveness or blessing. Those who take this view prefer declarations of forgiveness and blessings to be in the first person form (for example, 'The blessing of God . . . remain with us always'), thus expressing the solidarity of the speaker with those addressed. Indeed it is sometimes suggested that the 'you' form implies a sort of priestly separateness that is at variance with Methodist doctrine.

This is not the case. It belongs to the office of any leader of worship, lay or ordained, to proclaim the word of God. That word is declaratory: 'Thus says the Lord'. Those who use the 'you' form in declarations of forgiveness and blessings are set apart from those they address in precisely the way that they are set apart when they preach. They are set apart by the call of God to proclaim his word. To declare to others the forgiveness and blessing of God is in that sense an extension of the ministry of preaching. There is no suggestion that a person making such a declaration does not need God's forgiveness or blessing as much as those to whom the words are spoken. There is plenty of biblical precedent for second person utterances of this sort: for example, Numbers 6:24–26, Ruth 2:4 and Psalm 129:8.

Nevertheless, the Faith and Order Committee is aware that there is a variety of practice in Methodism. Though, in line with tradition, both the 1936 *Book of Offices* and the 1975 *Methodist Service Book* supply declarations of forgiveness, dismissals and blessings in the 'you' form, the Committee is aware that, in practice, some leaders of worship alter 'you' to 'us'. The intention of the Motion was to enable both practices to be 'owned' in the new service book.

The report then went on to say how the Faith and Order Committee proposed to deal with the issue. Its proposals were accepted by the Conference and have found their way into *The Methodist Worship Book*. The following paragraphs indicate how the matter has been addressed:

Declarations of Forgiveness

There is precedent both in the Bible and in the Christian liturgical tradition for declarations of forgiveness ('you') and prayers for forgiveness ('us'). The concerns of Motion 19 in this regard were met in a number of ways.

In many cases, a single text, which is unmistakably a quotation of Christ's words, is supplied. For example, in 'Holy Communion for Advent', we find (p. 118):

'I am making all things new', says the Lord.
This is Christ's gracious word:
'Your sins are forgiven.'
Amen. Thanks be to God.

Occasionally, italicized alternatives are offered, such as the following from 'Holy Communion for the Easter Season' (p. 161):

May the living God
raise *you/us* from despair,
give *you/us* victory over sin
and set *you/us* free in Christ.

Less frequently, completely different texts have been printed as alternatives, as in 'Holy Communion for Lent and Passiontide' (p. 149):

EITHER

The almighty and most
　　merciful God
grant you pardon,
forgiveness of all your sins,
time for true repentance
and amendment of life,
and the grace and comfort of
　　the Holy Spirit.

OR

May almighty God
have mercy on us,
forgive us our sins,
and keep us in life eternal.

Blessings

'Us' blessings have been much rarer in authorized Methodist liturgical texts than 'us' prayers for forgiveness, and have never been offered as alternatives but have occurred on their own in a minority of services, with the more general 'you' blessings appearing on their own in the majority. Nevertheless, *The Methodist Worship Book* has met the concerns of Motion 19 in the following ways:

Italicized alternatives have been printed in almost every case. For example, the Blessing in 'Holy Communion for Pentecost and Times of Renewal in the Life of the Church' reads (p. 184):

> The Spirit of truth lead *you/us* into all truth,
> give *you/us* grace to confess
> that Jesus Christ is Lord,
> and to proclaim the word and works of God;
> and the blessing of God,
> Spirit, Son, and Father,
> remain with *you/us* always.

More rarely, different texts are provided as alternatives, as in 'Holy Communion during Ordinary Seasons (Third Service)' (p. 220):

EITHER	OR
The Lord bless you and keep you; the Lord make his face to 　shine on you and be gracious to you; the Lord look on you with 　kindness and give you peace.	God be gracious to us 　and bless us, and make his face to 　shine upon us.

Dismissals

Dismissals could not be treated in the same sort of way as blessings or declarations of forgiveness. Their structure makes the use of italicized alternatives difficult. Nor did the Faith and Order Committee believe that to supply alternative texts in parallel columns would be appropriate. Dismissals, as their name suggests, are a proper extension of the prophetic preaching ministry – a sending out of the worshipping community into the world. Most dismissals, therefore, are in the imperative mood, as in 'Morning, Afternoon, or Evening Services (First Service)' (p. 38):

Go in peace to love and serve the Lord.
In the name of Christ. Amen.

Other dismissals, however, have a first person pronoun subject and a verb in the indicative mood. This can be illustrated by 'Morning, Afternoon, or Evening Services (Second Service)' (p. 50):

**We go into the world
to walk in God's light,
to rejoice in God's love
and to reflect God's glory. Amen.**

By adopting the methods described in the preceding paragraphs, the compilers of *The Methodist Worship Book* sought to accommodate two very different views about declarations of forgiveness, blessings and dismissals. The proposer of the original Motion pronounced himself well satisfied.

Historic Sources

Many worshippers may be unaware of how much of what is said and done in worship has been handed down through the centuries. They know, of course, that Bible readings and Psalms are ancient texts and that some of our hymns and canticles are very old, but they may be surprised to learn that many other familiar prayers, words and phrases can be traced back through many generations. There will be references throughout this book to several major historic sources and so a brief account of them may be helpful at this point.

We rarely know for sure, in the case of ancient prayers, precisely how old they are and who wrote them, but their first known appearance can often be identified. In the early Middle Ages, in the Western Church, a number of liturgical 'books' began to appear, the most important of which (for our purposes) were the 'sacramentaries'. A sacramentary was a book used by a priest. It contained all the texts that were required by a person presiding at the Lord's Supper, at Baptism, and sometimes at other acts of worship. The major sacramentaries that we shall consider were named after Bishops of Rome, though this should not be taken to mean that the person named necessarily had any part in their production.

The Leonine Sacramentary

The Leonine Sacramentary is the oldest known book of this type, although it is nowhere near as comprehensive as the later sacramentaries. Named after the fifth-century Pope Leo I, this document is thought to date from around AD 600 and to reflect the practice of the Church in Rome.

The Gelasian Sacramentary

It is likely that the Gelasian Sacramentary originated in France in the middle of the eighth century and that it has no real connection with the fifth-century Pope after whom it is named, though there is evidence to suggest that it contains some material that reflects practice in Rome at the time of its compilation. It is far more wide-ranging than the Leonine Sacramentary, and many collects which are still in use today can be traced back to it.

The Gregorian Sacramentary

Despite its name, which associates it with Gregory the Great (sixth century), the Gregorian Sacramentary cannot be regarded as older than the late eighth or early ninth century, slightly later than the Gelasian Sacramentary. Like the latter, it includes many texts, especially of collects, versions of which appear in many modern service books.

In the later medieval period, missals began to appear. They combined the material from sacramentaries with that contained in lectionaries (full texts of appointed readings) and other material, to provide complete texts to be used at Holy Communion. At this time, there was some degree of variation, reflecting local traditions, in the way in which the service was celebrated in the West, though its general shape and content were established. Occasional attempts to impose liturgical uniformity (usually for political reasons) were unsuccessful.

The Sarum Missal

Variations in liturgical practice extended to different regions; not only might there be differences, mainly minor, between what was done in Italy and what happened in France, but even within the same country there was no absolute uniformity. This was true also of England, but one particular missal, that of the Diocese of Salisbury (Sarum), was very influential and widely used. The Sarum Missal was dominant in the south of England on the eve of the Reformation, and it was generally by way of that missal that the contents of the earlier sacramentaries and other liturgical books were transmitted to the 'Prayer Book' tradition.

The Book of Common Prayer

The liturgical history of the English-speaking world in the last 500 years has been dominated by successive editions of *The Book of Common Prayer*. As the previous paragraphs have suggested, the 'Prayer Book' tradition was strongly influenced by the medieval usage of Sarum, which was itself indebted to the sacramentaries and other liturgical books of an earlier age.

One of the fruits of the sixteenth-century Protestant Reformation in England was liturgical reform. At first this was fairly conservative; the earliest version of *The Book of Common Prayer*, which was published in 1549, did not satisfy many Reformers, who had been influenced by what was happening elsewhere in Europe. They wished to see a greater reformation in matters of doctrine and ceremony.

The guiding spirit behind the 1549 book and its much more 'Protestant' successor of 1552 was Thomas Cranmer, Archbishop of Canterbury, whose facility in writing and revising liturgical texts has become legendary. There will be numerous references to Cranmer in the pages which follow.

During the reign of Mary I, the pre-Cranmerian rites were restored to use and the legislation which had authorized the use of the 1552 book was repealed, but, following the accession of Elizabeth I in 1558, *The Book of Common Prayer* in its 1552 form, with some minor emendations, was restored. Further minor changes were made in 1604, and then in 1662, when *The Book of Common Prayer* was again revised after the restoration of the monarchy.

For two and a half centuries, the 1662 book held sway in the Church of England, without any serious attempt being made to revise it. John Wesley, who had grown up with it, declared:

> I believe that there is no Liturgy in the world, either in ancient or modern language, which breathes more of solid, Scriptural, rational piety than the Common Prayer of the Church of England; and though the main of it was compiled more than two hundred years ago, yet is the language of it not only pure, but strong and elegant in the highest degree.

In 1784 Wesley made a fairly conservative revision of parts of the 1662 book for the Methodists in North America. 'Our Venerable Father's Abridgement', as it was often known, came into use in Britain, and successive Methodist service books remained strongly under the influence of *The Book of Common Prayer*. This was true of *The Book of Offices* (1936), published shortly after Methodist Union, and it was not until the publication of *The Methodist Service Book* (1975) that indebtedness to the Prayer Book tradition began to wane. It certainly did not disappear, however; nor has it yet disappeared.

Within the Church of England, early in the twentieth century, there was a widespread desire for a revision of the 1662 book, but there was no unanimity about the direction in which it should be revised. An attempt in 1928 to get a revised version of *The Book of Common Prayer* authorized by Parliament – a necessary step at that time – proved unsuccessful. There will be references later to the 1928 revision, which was influential despite its lack of parliamentary approval, and which inspired revisions in other parts of the Anglican Communion, where no such approval was required.

5

Daily Prayer

The first liturgical section of *The Methodist Worship Book* provides material for use by individuals or small groups meeting for daily devotions. It is not intended for public worship on Sundays. No previous Methodist service book had made similar provision. ('The Order for Morning Prayer', which appeared in most Methodist service books from 1784 to 1936, was intended for use in public worship.) There had, however, been numerous requests to the Faith and Order Committee for services which could be used by individuals and groups on weekdays and the draft versions of 'Daily Prayer' were well received.

'Daily Prayer' begins with sentences of Scripture, appropriate for the seasons of the Christian year and for other occasions. One of these sentences may be said at no. 2 of 'Prayer in the Morning' or 'Prayer in the Evening'.

'Prayer in the Morning' and 'Prayer in the Evening' are simple and straightforward 'offices', acts of prayer and praise intended for daily devotion. The Introduction to this section of the book very briefly explains that daily acts of worship have a long history and may perhaps have occurred in the time of the early Church. The combination of praise (in the form of Psalms and canticles), prayer and the reading of Bible passages, in acts of worship to be performed at specified times each day, can be traced back with confidence to the early days of monastic communities (from the fourth century onwards), though there were other influences too. By the Middle Ages, such communities had eight 'offices', in addition to Holy Communion, which were used on a daily basis. In *The Book of Common Prayer* (1549) these offices were reduced to two, Morning and Evening Prayer.

In preparing 'Prayer in the Morning' and 'Prayer in the Evening', the Liturgical Sub-Committee sought to ensure that these services should be flexible and adaptable, so that they could be used in different ways according to circumstances. So, for example, 'Prayer in the Morning' could be used, exactly as printed, by a commuter travelling by train, without any other book being needed, since prayers, Psalms, Bible readings, hymns and canticles are supplied in the text. Not everyone, however, would want to say the same Psalm every morning, or to read the same biblical passage every Wednesday, for example. So other possibilities are suggested, which could be helpful to those with access to Bibles or hymn books. The rubrics of these two services repeatedly encourage the use of other material, while invariably supplying a 'default' text: 'This or some other prayer'; 'Either one of the following or a reading from scripture selected freely or according to some other scheme'; and so on.

'Prayer in the Morning' and 'Prayer in the Evening' share a common structure:

Opening Sentences

Seasonal or Occasional Sentences

Sentences for the Day

Prayers of Penitence

Canticle or Hymn

The Prayer of the Morning or Evening

Psalm

Reading from Scripture

Canticle

Prayers

Concluding Sentences.

This is the traditional 'daily office' in its simplest form. Indeed, as we shall see, these two services are an interesting blend of the traditional and the modern.

Prayer in the Morning

The opening sentences (1), based on Psalm 51.15, were included in Vigils, the first office of the day, by St Benedict in the sixth century, continued to be associated with this office in the Western Church, and were included in Morning Prayer in *The Book of Common Prayer* (1662).

They are followed, during Eastertide, by the appropriate acclamations (2), whose origins are lost in the mists of time. They are certainly Byzantine, and found their way into several Western liturgies in the twentieth century. At other times an appropriate Scripture sentence may be said. Each day has its own set of Scripture sentences (3) in addition. *Gloria Patri* (4) and prayers of penitence (5) may follow, though no text is provided for the latter.

The canticle *Venite* (Psalm 95) (6) or 'Christ, whose glory fills the skies' or some other hymn may then be sung or said. *Venite* has been associated with morning offices since their earliest days; the translation in *The Methodist Worship Book* is the work of a member of the Liturgical Sub-Committee. The provision that a hymn may be sung instead of the canticle at this point gives recognition to the part that hymnody plays in Methodist spirituality and it may make the service more accessible to some people who are unfamiliar with traditional offices. No apology needs to be made for the inclusion of this great hymn by Charles Wesley.

The Prayer of the Morning (7) was written for *The Methodist Worship Book*. It is followed by a Psalm (8) and by a reading from Scripture (9). 'Default' texts are supplied both for the Psalm and for the Bible reading, for the reasons indicated above. Care was taken to ensure that a reasonably representative sample of Scripture was made available in this way: one passage is drawn from the Law, one from the Prophets, one from the Wisdom literature; two from the Epistles, and two from the Gospels.

Benedictus, or *Te Deum Laudamus*, or some other canticle (10) follows the Bible reading. *Benedictus* is the Song of Zechariah (Luke 1.68–79) and has been associated with prayer in the morning for well over 1,000 years. By accident rather than by design, there is a deviation from the English Language Liturgical Consultation translation in line 20, where 'heaven' has been substituted for 'on high'.

No one knows the origin of *Te Deum Laudamus*, which was first associated with morning prayer in the sixth century. It has sometimes been attributed to St Ambrose (339–97), but there is no firm evidence for this. Unfortunately, another unintentional alteration has been made to an ecumenical text in line 35 of *Te Deum Laudamus*, where 'we put' appears instead of 'we have put'.

After these traditional texts come some newly-written prayers (11), which begin with an invitation, identifying appropriate topics for intercession, before the prayers are gathered together in a request that God will answer them. The Lord's Prayer (12), printed here as it is throughout *The Methodist Worship Book* in two columns, is followed by a lovely new prayer (13) in which the new day is offered to God. The final sentences (14) are part of a responsive conclusion, used in various daily offices since at least the ninth century.

Prayer in the Evening

'Prayer in the Evening', as has already been observed, follows the same pattern as 'Prayer in the Morning' and, like the latter, it begins with three sets of sentences (1, 2, 3) and *Gloria Patri* (4). In this service, however, a prayer of penitence (5) is printed in the text, followed by a declaration of forgiveness (1 John 1.9). The prayer itself, though a new composition, draws on some familiar phrases from older prayers.

The first canticle (6) is *Jubilate* (Psalm 100), for which the ancient hymn 'Hail, gladdening Light', or some other hymn, may be substituted. The former represents something of a break with tradition, for *Jubilate* has normally been associated with morning offices. The translation is, once again, the work of a member of the Liturgical Sub-Committee. The hymn is ancient, certainly dating back to the fourth century and probably to an earlier period, when it was sung during evening prayer as the lamps were lit.

Two texts are supplied for the Prayer of the Evening (7); both are new compositions. As in 'Prayer in the Morning', the Psalm (8) is followed by a Scripture reading (9) for which seven passages, one for each day of the week, are printed. In this selection, the New Testament is much better represented than the Old, from which only one reading is drawn.

Magnificat, or *Nunc Dimittis*, or some other canticle follows. Like *Benedictus*, these printed canticles are derived from Luke's Gospel; they are, respectively, the Song of Mary and the Song of Simeon. Both have been associated with evening offices from at least the sixth century.

A fine set of new responsive prayers (11), the Lord's Prayer (12) and a lovely new prayer for the ending of the day (13) are followed (14) by Scripture sentences, which have traditionally been associated with 'Compline', a service of Night Prayer, or by the dialogue,

Let us bless the Lord.
Thanks be to God.

The final sentence (15) in this service has been used in many liturgical contexts; it can be traced back to the medieval office of Prime, though the last phrase is a much later addition. The inclusion of this sentence caused some controversy at the 1998 Conference, when an unsuccessful attempt was made to have it removed or modified, on the grounds that it can be interpreted as a prayer for the departed. At the close of the day, however, it is good to be reminded of the communion of saints and to pray that members of the Church on earth, like the faithful departed, may 'rest in peace and rise in glory'.

6

Morning, Afternoon, or Evening Services

This section of *The Methodist Worship Book*, like the one that precedes it, is an innovation, for nothing quite like it has appeared in any previous Methodist service book. It is true that *The Methodist Service Book* supplied an outline structure for what it called 'The Sunday Service without the Lord's Supper', but 'Morning, Afternoon, or Evening Services' offers much more.

Considerable debate took place in the Liturgical Sub-Committee about this section. Should it consist simply of 'resource material' – a selection of prayers of adoration, confession, and so on, together with other material, such as Scripture sentences – or should complete orders of service be provided? Some members of the Sub-Committee felt that it was foreign to the Methodist ethos to provide full liturgies for 'services of the word' or 'preaching services'. Others believed that, though it had not been done before, this did not necessarily mean that such liturgies would not be welcomed and valued.

It was decided to issue for trial use and comment a booklet entitled *Preaching Services (or Services of the Word)*. This appeared in October 1994 and contained two full orders of service, supplemented by other resource material. Comment was invited on this format, as well as on the content of the material itself, though relatively little comment was forthcoming. In the end, the Liturgical Sub-Committee took the view that this section of *The Methodist Worship Book* should resemble other sections as closely as possible, and consequently two complete orders of service were provided, together with some additional seasonal material.

A second issue, not resolved until the preparation of *The Methodist Worship Book* was nearing completion, was what this section was going to be called. It was widely felt that *The Methodist Service Book*'s title, 'The Sunday Service without the Lord's Supper', was altogether too negative. The term 'preaching services', which was used in the 1994 draft, is quite widely employed, but suffers from the disadvantage that it seems to place exclusive emphasis upon one element of worship – the preaching. A similar criticism can be levelled against another possible candidate, 'services of the word'. In the absence of anything better, the rather mundane title 'Morning and Evening Services' was briefly adopted, though with some misgivings. It was feared that the first service would mistakenly be thought to be designed solely for mornings and the second for evenings, whereas either is suitable for any time of day. This potential problem, was, however, rapidly overcome with the realization that there are many churches, not least in rural areas, that have services on Sunday afternoons. So the title became 'Morning, Afternoon, or Evening Services'.

Like 'Daily Prayer', 'Morning, Afternoon, or Evening Services' is capable of being used in a variety of ways. Either of the two liturgies, each of which contains at least two sets of prayers of approach, adoration, confession, thanksgiving, intercession and dedication, could be used as printed, from beginning to end, with leader and congregation alike using the book. But the services may be used in other ways; the congregation could be invited to turn to *The Methodist Worship Book* only at certain points (for example, for the prayers of thanksgiving); the leader alone could read prayers from the book, or could invite the congregation to join in those prayers where a single response is repeated a number of times; some material could be drawn from both printed services in the same act of worship; and so on.

The two services in this section have a common structure:

Preparation
Ministry of the Word
Response
Dismissal.

This is a slightly developed form of the structure proposed in *The Methodist Service Book*, where the Dismissal was incorporated into the Response. Its promotion to being a division of the service in its own right in *The Methodist Worship Book* is an expression of the conviction that the 'sending forth' at the end of the formal act of worship is as important in its own way as the 'gathering' at the start.

Though the overall structure of the two services is the same, however, they differ somewhat in points of detail, as the following outlines make clear:

First Service

Preparation

Sentences
Hymn
Prayer of approach
Prayer of adoration
Prayer of confession and
    declaration of forgiveness
The collect
The Lord's Prayer (if not later)
Hymn

Ministry of the Word

Two or three readings from
    Scripture with psalms,
    hymns, etc.
Sermon
Affirmation of Faith
Hymn

Second Service

Preparation

Sentences
Hymn
Prayer of approach
Prayer of adoration
The collect
The Lord's Prayer (if not later)
Hymn

Ministry of the Word

Two or three readings from
    Scripture with psalms,
    hymns, etc.
Sermon

Response

Prayers of thanksgiving
Prayers of intercession
The Lord's Prayer (if not
   earlier or later)
Offering and prayer of
   dedication
The Lord's Prayer (if not
   earlier)

Response

Prayer of confession and
   declaration of forgiveness
The Peace
Offering and prayer of
   dedication
Hymn
Prayers of thanksgiving
Prayers of intercession
The Lord's Prayer (if not
   earlier)

Dismissal

Hymn
Blessing
Dismissal

Dismissal

Hymn
Blessing
Dismissal

Each order of service contains some items which might be included in a 'service of the word' on occasion, but not invariably. In the First Service, the Affirmation of Faith falls into this category; in the Second Service, the Peace. The most significant difference between the two orders, however, is in the contents of the Preparation and of the Response.

The First Service puts the prayer of confession and declaration of forgiveness in the Preparation. This may be regarded as its most usual and natural place: as we approach God and offer our adoration, we are moved to penitence and ask and receive forgiveness. Then we proceed to hear God's word and to respond. Confession and declaration of forgiveness are positioned in the Preparation in almost all the services of Holy Communion, as well as in the first 'preaching service'. But the Second Service places them in the Response, as an indication that there may be occasions when it is more appropriate to seek and receive God's forgiveness as an immediate response to the reading and proclamation of God's word.

Another difference between the two services is that the prayers of thanksgiving and intercession precede the offering and prayer of dedication in the First Service, whereas they follow them in the second. There is no great significance in this variation; all these acts are appropriate acts of response, but the order in which they come is not of special importance.

It was the Faith and Order Committee's intention that the First Service should indicate that the Lord's Prayer should follow either the prayers of intercession or the prayer of dedication. In the Second Service, it was to follow the prayers of intercession. Thus the Lord's Prayer would always be in the Response. An amendment which came before the Conference Revision Committee, however, urged that provision be made for the Lord's Prayer to be included in the Preparation in both services, and this was approved by the Revision Committee. Thus the First Service suggests three possible positions for the Lord's Prayer; the Second Service suggests two. Much the best policy, nevertheless, is to include the Lord's Prayer as an act of Response. It is the greatest of all prayers and deserves to come as the climax of prayer in response to the proclamation of God's word.

Special mention should be made of the inclusion, in each of the two services, of prayers of thanksgiving within the Response. Thanksgiving is probably the most neglected element of prayer in Methodist 'preaching services'. Sometimes it is confused with adoration and included, often almost in passing, in the Preparation. All too frequently, it is omitted altogether. The prayers of response are then reduced to prayers of intercession. One of the reasons for the neglect of thanksgiving may be that, in services of Holy Communion, prayers of intercession, but not of thanksgiving, closely follow the sermon. But in Holy Communion, of course, the great prayer of thanksgiving is yet to come, as part of the re-enactment of the actions of Jesus at the Last Supper (of which more will be written in Chapter Eight).

The frequent absence of thanksgiving is to be regretted. The reading and preaching of the word of God should result in a variety of responses, perhaps the most important of which should be thankfulness for the mighty acts of God in creation and redemption. It is to be hoped that the provision of prayers of thanksgiving in the two 'Morning, Afternoon, or Evening Services', which are offered as models as well as complete services in their own right, will help to restore this important element of prayer to Methodist 'preaching services'.

A somewhat unusual feature of *The Methodist Worship Book* is particularly obvious in 'Morning, Afternoon, or Evening Services'. This is the inclusion of a letter (A, B, C, etc.) before prayers, readings, blessings and at other places where choices need to be made. It resulted from a proposal to the Revision Committee and undoubtedly helps users of the book to find their way between alternatives or among options.

First Service

A choice of opening sentences (1) is provided, both in the main body of the service and in the Resource Material (pp. 52–5). It is much better to begin an act of public worship by reading sentences of Scripture (and better still if the sentences can be said responsively, by leader and congregation) than to start with some well-intentioned friendly greeting, such as 'Good morning!' Scripture sentences set a proper tone; the People of God have gathered as a community to worship God. The other sort of greeting can be offered on any occasion, such as a chance encounter in the street; to begin a service in this way is to run the risk of reducing worship to an encounter between human beings.

Two prayers of approach (3) are printed. The first (3A), written for *The Methodist Worship Book*, asks that the act of worship may be worthy of its purpose. The second prayer is taken from the Church of England's *Lent, Holy Week, Easter* (1984, 1986) which, incidentally, is incorrectly called *Lent, Holy Week and Easter* in the Acknowledgements (pp. 602 and 605). This prayer begins with the *Trisagion*, an ancient hymn from the Orthodox tradition. After a silence, the prayer continues with a request that those present may worship God with all their 'heart and mind and strength'.

It may be noted that, whichever prayer is to be said, the leader speaks before the congregation joins in. This is one of a number of devices employed in *The Methodist Worship Book* to try to avoid the need for leaders of worship to say such things as 'We shall now say prayer 3A on page 27', which rather detract from the atmosphere of communal celebration. In this instance, because the leader's opening words differ in prayers A and B, the congregation does not need to be told which prayer is being said.

The first prayer of adoration (4A) is an interesting example of the way in which the compilers of liturgies 'borrow' from one another. The Acknowledgements indicate (p. 602) that this prayer is an emendation of a prayer from the Australian *Uniting in Worship* (1988). Though it does appear in that book, its first appearance was in *Companion to the Lectionary, Volume 3* (1983), edited by the present writer, for which it was written by Martyn Atkins.

The second prayer of adoration (4B) comes from Norman Wallwork's *Prayers for the Sunday Preaching Service* (1987). It is a fine example of a thoroughly Trinitarian prayer, both in content and in structure.

From adoration, the service moves to confession (5). Here a different device is employed to enable the congregation to know which prayer is being used; different introductory sentences are provided for each of the three prayers. All these prayers are the work of the Liturgical Sub-Committee, though the first especially reflects much older prayers in some of its phrases. The second prayer (5B) has the distinction of being the first example of the use in *The Methodist Worship Book* of a translation of the ancient Greek prayer *Kyrie eleison* ('Lord, have mercy'). These words are also used in many other places in the book. Here *Kyrie eleison* is used almost as it was at its first known appearance in the fourth century – as a congregational response within a set of prayers. The third prayer (5C) is unusual in that it is introduced by words which are more commonly spoken as a declaration of forgiveness (as indeed they are elsewhere in the book). In each of the prayers there is provision for silence.

Ideally, the first group of prayers in this service will conclude with the collect of the day (6) or another suitable prayer, but the

Lord's Prayer may be said after it. The Conference Revision Committee's decision to sanction the possibility of saying the Lord's Prayer at this point has already been discussed.

The Ministry of the Word follows, with two or three readings from Scripture, and maybe Psalms, canticles, hymns or periods of silence (9). After the sermon (10), there is a very short Affirmation of Faith (11). It is open to question whether it was appropriate to introduce this Affirmation with the words 'Let us confess the faith of the Church', when very similar words are used for the Nicene Creed in other services (for example, on p. 135). The Affirmation is at best a summary of the faith of the Church; indeed, it is little more than a confession of belief in the three Persons of the Trinity. Presumably this point did not occur to the present writer at the time when it was agreed that the introductory words should be included; or maybe contrary arguments prevailed, which have since been forgotten!

The Response begins with prayers of thanksgiving (13). The first (13A), like 4A, is derived from *Prayers for the Sunday Preaching Service*. The second (13B) is based on a prayer from *The Methodist Service Book*, where it was printed as a model for what prayers of thanksgiving should contain. The revised version allows for much more congregational participation than the original.

The first prayer of intercession (14A) will also seem familiar to those who remember *The Methodist Service Book*; it is a version of one of the sets of intercessions provided in 'The Sunday Service'. That set of intercessions was itself an adaptation of a prayer from New Zealand. Yet another version of it appears on pp. 290–1 of *The Methodist Worship Book*.

The link with *The Methodist Service Book* is maintained by the second set of intercessions (14B), a lightly revised form of the intercessions which were set out in the main body of 'The Sunday Service'. These beautifully crafted prayers had stood the test of time (apart from their exclusive language which has, of course, been amended) and it was felt that they should be included somewhere in the new book.

The best possible place for the Lord's Prayer (15) is now

reached, though it may be deferred until after the Offering (provided that it has not, by some mischance, been said earlier in the service). Two short prayers of dedication (16) are supplied for use after the Offering; these are new compositions.

Of the two blessings provided, the first (19A) may be preceded by a seasonal introduction (pp. 57–9). The second (19B) is borrowed from the Church of Scotland's *Book of Common Order* (1994).

Second Service

In the Second Service, the same suggestions are made about opening sentences (1) as in the First Service. Otherwise, no spoken text in the First Service, apart from the Lord's Prayer and the first form of the blessing, is repeated in the second.

The first prayer of approach (3A) is a revised version of a prayer from *Uniting in Worship* (1988). The second (3B) is derived from *Celebrating Common Prayer* (1992), a Franciscan publication which has already exerted significant influence on other worship books, not least the Church of England's *Common Worship* (2000). The Liturgical Sub-Committee was responsible for the writing of the first prayer of adoration (4A), which praises the God who, as Father, Son and Holy Spirit, acts in love towards his creation.

The second prayer of adoration (4B) is attributed in the Acknowledgements (p. 602) to *Uniting in Worship*. Though this attribution is correct, some years before *Uniting in Worship* was published an earlier version of the prayer had already appeared in Britain in *Companion to the Lectionary, Volume 3* (1983), for which it was written by the Australian liturgist Robert Gribben.

In this service, as we have already noted, confession is included in the Response. *Uniting in Worship* is the source of the first prayer (10A). The structure and some of the text of the second (10B) were inspired by a prayer in *The Iona Community Worship Book* (1991), the original form of which can be traced back to George MacLeod, the founder of the Iona Community.

It has an interesting and unusual form, in that the leader of worship first makes his or her confession to God and to the people, who then pray that he or she may be forgiven. After that, the reverse happens: the people make their confession and the leader prays that they may be forgiven. The occasional use of this prayer may be a salutary reminder that those who normally make declarations of forgiveness are themselves sinners who need to be forgiven.

The Peace (11) is usually associated with the Lord's Supper, with which indeed its earliest known liturgical appearance is linked, but it is thought that it may also have been included in other early Christian gatherings.

The first prayer of dedication (12A) after the offering begins with a quotation from 1 Chronicles 29.11, 14. The first sentence of the second (12B) is based on a prayer from the *Book of Common Order* (1994) of the Church of Scotland. The rest of the prayer is the work of the Liturgical Sub-Committee.

For the first of the prayers of thanksgiving (14A) *The Methodist Worship Book* is indebted to the *Supplemental Liturgical Resource No. 1* of the Presbyterian Church of the United States of America. The second prayer (14B) is the Liturgical Sub-Committee's own composition.

Another text that has stood the test of time is offered as the first prayer of intercession (15A). It was included in Holy Communion, Rite A, in the Church of England's *The Alternative Service Book* (1980) and thus had to bear frequent repetition. (It had, in fact, already been in regular use for some years prior to 1980, having first appeared in the 'Series 2' service [1966] and subsequent services which preceded *The Alternative Service Book*.) It has survived, much altered, to be included in *Common Worship* (2000). The version in *The Methodist Worship Book* allows for biddings on specific topics, followed by periods of silent prayer, leading into spoken prayers and responses. It is a good illustration of the range of concerns that ought to be included in prayers of intercession.

The form of the second set of intercessions (15A) is very different. Here, the Liturgical Sub-Committee has provided no fewer than ten short biddings, followed by *Kyrie eleison*, before a final collect. In place of the usual dismissal by the leader, words of commitment spoken by the whole congregation (19) bring this service to a close.

Guidance for Ordering a Morning, Afternoon, or Evening Service

The two complete orders of worship are followed by 'Guidance for Ordering a Morning, Afternoon, or Evening Service'. This consists of an outline of what such a service should or may contain. On the whole its structure corresponds more closely to that of the First Service than that of the second. The 'Guidance' was added at the Revision Committee stage, in response to an amendment. Those who argued for its inclusion had in mind congregations to whom a 'book culture' is foreign. It was said that, though such congregations would be unlikely ever to use the material in the two full services, an outline giving guidance to the leaders of worship among them would be helpful.

Resource Material

This section of the book concludes with eight pages of 'Resource Material' containing opening sentences, seasonal material for prayers of thanksgiving and seasonal introductions to the blessing, in recognition of the way in which appreciation of the Christian year has developed among Methodists. It seemed sensible, in gathering together this resource material, to draw upon the work already ably done by others; *The Alternative Service Book* (1980) is its principal source.

As the comments above will have made clear, although some of the prayers and other material in 'Morning, Afternoon, or Evening Services' were written specially for *The Methodist Worship Book*, a good deal of material came from other sources from around the world. In many cases, alterations, small or large, were made before 'borrowed' texts were included in *The Methodist Worship Book*. This is an example of a common practice among liturgists, who, as we have seen, are great 'borrowers' of texts, but can rarely resist the urge to adapt, rewrite and 'improve'.

7

Entry into the Church

'Entry into the Church' was the title given in *The Methodist Service Book* (1975) to the section which contained 'initiation services' – Baptism, Confirmation and Reception into Membership. The title is retained in *The Methodist Worship Book*.

The Introduction (pp. 60f.) is an important theological statement about Baptism, Confirmation and Reception into Membership. Then follow no fewer than five services. The reader may wonder why so many services are needed, especially since they have many texts in common.

The reason for such abundant provision is that there are many different circumstances in which initiation services may be required. Three of them are relatively straightforward. First, the Baptism of young children is undoubtedly the initiation service most frequently encountered in most local churches. Second, the Confirmation and Reception into Membership of those who have previously been baptized will also be familiar. Third, less frequently perhaps, there will be the Baptism of 'those who are able to answer for themselves', usually followed immediately by their Confirmation and Reception into Membership. A service is provided for each of these three. But these are not the only possibilities.

Occasionally, a whole family (or some other combination of adults and young children) is to be baptized, with those who are able to answer for themselves proceeding immediately to Confirmation and Reception. A service in these circumstances, reminiscent of the household baptisms to which the New Testament refers, will include elements of the first and third services mentioned above. Or it may happen that a young child is to be baptized at a service during which a person previously baptized is to be confirmed and received. There are further possibilities; 'in exceptional circumstances and for good reason' (pp. 70 and 82) the Confirmation of those who have been baptized when able to answer for themselves may be delayed.

There was a time when the Liturgical Sub-Committee believed that it might be possible to provide for all these possibilities within a single service. Carefully written rubrics, it was hoped, would enable ministers and congregations to find the parts of the service which were required on any given occasion and to pass over those that were not needed. A draft was produced which seemed admirably to fulfil these objectives. Wisely, however, the Liturgical Sub-Committee resolved to test out the theory. In the most extraordinary two-hour period of any of their meetings the members of the Sub-Committee acted out a number of initiation services using the draft. They 'simulated' the Baptism of a young child; there followed an 'able to answer' Baptism; and so on. For all these 'simulations', the Liturgical Sub-Committee used the same draft service with its multiple options and necessarily complex rubrics. The result was chaotic. Neither the person playing the part of the minister nor those pretending to present themselves for Baptism or Confirmation or their child for Baptism could find their way through the service without a great deal of confusion, the inclusion of wrong sections or the omission of parts that should have been included. There was much mirth, coupled with something approaching desperation. What had seemed so plausible in theory proved to be impossible in practice.

Nevertheless, the Liturgical Sub-Committee was reluctant to abandon the attempt to produce a single, comprehensive service. If only the rubrics were improved, it was argued, all would be well. A revised draft was produced, but the subsequent 'simulations' were no more successful than the first. It was clear beyond all reasonable doubt that several services would be needed.

The detailed Notes (pp. 62f., 76f., 88, 97, 103) which precede each service indicate the precise circumstances in which that service should be used. There should be no room for uncertainty as to which service is appropriate for any given circumstances.

Four of the five services include Baptism. The other service is
for Confirmation only. Each of the five services contains the
relevant parts of what is essentially a common structure and
there are many texts which appear in most of the services. The
common structure is shown in the table on pp. 62f., from which
hymns have been omitted.

The structure of all these services is of particular interest
because an important theological principle has influenced it. This
principle concerns the promises which are made during every
initiation service.

In earlier Methodist service books, candidates for Baptism, or
their parent(s) and godparent(s), were asked to make various
promises before Baptism took place. Similarly, candidates for
Confirmation and Reception into Membership made promises
before being confirmed and received. The impression may have
been given that Baptism and/or Confirmation was administered
in response to the making of these promises. If so, that is regrettable, because Methodist theology, following the lead of John
Wesley, places much emphasis upon 'prevenient grace' – God's
grace which is extended to us before we can make any response
to it. The new services are an eloquent testimony to our belief in
prevenient grace. Baptism is administered, a sign of God's love
and acceptance; only then, and in response to the divine act, are
promises made. Something similar happens in Confirmation.

It is true that candidates for either Baptism or Confirmation
(or both) must request Baptism and/or Confirmation, or, in the
case of young children, Baptism must be requested for them, and
that, in all the services, an affirmation of faith precedes the central act. The faith of the Church is affirmed by candidates or their
parent(s) and by the whole company of those present. That faith
is the context in which a Baptism or a Confirmation takes place,
and its affirmation properly comes at this point in the services.
But promises, such as those to ensure that children are nurtured
within the Christian community, or to witness to the good news
by word and deed, are reserved until later, when the minister
introduces them with the words:

I ask you now to respond to God's love and grace (to your children) by making these promises.

The Services which Include Baptism

The four services which include Baptism will be discussed together; with all textual references being to the first service (pp. 63–75).

After an optional hymn (1), each service starts with a Declaration (2), which, like many of the texts in 'Entry into the Church', is an original composition. The fact that the same Declaration, the same baptismal prayer (the thanksgiving over the water) and various other words are said in all the services, irrespective of whether the Baptism is of young children, or of those able to answer for themselves, or of both, is quite deliberate. It emphasizes that Baptism is Baptism, whatever the age of its recipients. There is no such thing as a theology of 'infant' Baptism or a theology of 'adult' Baptism. There is only a theology of Baptism.

The Declaration makes clear that it is God who takes the initiative in Baptism, by reaching out to the world in love and inviting our response. Two passages of Scripture are incorporated into the Declaration – the 'Great Commission' (Matthew 28.18ff.) and part of Peter's sermon on the Day of Pentecost (Acts 2.38f.).

Requests for Baptism (3 and 4) now follow. The minister asks the candidates (or the parent[s] of young children) how, 'having heard these things', they respond to the offer of God's grace. Candidates who are able to answer reply: 'I thank God, and ask to be baptized.' Parents of young children, however, must do their best to select the right words from what is surely the least user-friendly sentence in *The Methodist Worship Book*:

We/I thank God, and ask that *our/my child/children* be baptized.

The Baptism of those who are able to answer for themselves, and of young children, with Confirmation and Reception into Membership	The Baptism of those who are able to answer for themselves, with Confirmation and Reception into Membership	The Baptism of young children	Confirmation and Reception into Membership	The Baptism of young children, with Confirmation and Reception into Membership
Declaration	Declaration	Declaration		Declaration
Request for Baptism	Request for Baptism	Request for Baptism		Request for Baptism
(Testimony)	(Testimony)			
Thanksgiving over the Water	Thanksgiving over the Water	Thanksgiving over the Water		Thanksgiving over the Water
Affirmation of Faith	Affirmation of Faith	Affirmation of Faith		Affirmation of Faith
Baptism	Baptism	Baptism		Baptism
Signing	Signing	Signing		Signing
(Giving of Candle)	(Giving of Candle)	(Giving of Candle)		(Giving of Candle)
Aaronic Blessing	Aaronic Blessing	Aaronic Blessing		Aaronic Blessing
Promises of parent(s) (and godparent[s])		Promises of parent(s) (and godparent[s])		Promises of parent(s) (and godparent[s])
Promise of the People in respect of newly-baptized children		Promise of the People		Promise of the People in respect of newly-baptized children

		Declaration	Declaration
		Prayer	Prayer
Request for Confirmation	Request for Confirmation	Request for Confirmation	Request for Confirmation
		(Testimony)	(Testimony)
		Affirmation of Faith	
Confirmation	Confirmation	Confirmation	Confirmation
Reception and Welcome	Reception and Welcome	Reception and Welcome	Reception and Welcome
Promises of those newly confirmed	Promises of those newly confirmed	Promises of those newly confirmed	Promises of those newly confirmed
Promise of the People in respect of those newly baptized and confirmed	Promise of the People	Promise of the People	Promise of the People in respect of those newly confirmed
Presentation of books/certificates	Presentation of books/certificates	Presentation of books/certificates	Presentation of books/certificates
Prayer	Prayer	Prayer	Prayer

Wise ministers will write out for the parent(s) what actually needs to be said at this point. The difficulty, of course, is that there may be one or more children of either one or two parents. The only way of avoiding the 'catch-all' answer printed above would have been to set out in full the four possible answers, and it is not self-evident that this method would have been any more helpful to parents than what is printed.

In the two services involving the Baptism of those able to answer, there is provision after the request for Baptism for a candidate to give personal testimony (5). The rubric is permissive: there is no requirement that a testimony should be given. It would be a more natural occurrence in some churches than in others.

The services envisage the possibility that either a font or a baptistry will be used. The services of Baptism in the draft edition of *The Methodist Worship Book* referred only to a font, the references to a baptistry being inserted by the Conference Revision Committee. Baptistries are exceedingly rare features of Methodist churches (if indeed they are to be found at all), though many Methodists now share in local ecumenical partnerships, some of which use buildings equipped with baptistries.

When a font is to be used, water is now poured into it 'in the sight of the people' (6). This was an innovation for Methodists in 1991 when another version of 'Entry into the Church' was authorized by the Conference as an alternative to the initiation services contained in *The Methodist Service Book*. The pouring, which is likely to be audible, as well as visible, to the congregation, is a reminder that sacraments make use of material things. This action may be compared with the taking of the bread and wine before the Great Prayer of Thanksgiving in Holy Communion.

The candidates and/or the parent(s) (and godparent[s]) then gather round or near the font or baptistry and the minister leads the prayer of thanksgiving over the water. This prayer, like many of its equivalents in other modern service books, stands in a tradition at least as old as the seventh century in that it exploits some of the rich biblical imagery about water (the waters at creation, the crossing of the Red Sea, the baptism of Jesus in the Jordan, his passing through the deep waters of death, his offer of 'living water'). Then follows a sort of baptismal *epiclesis*, as prayer is offered for a pouring out of the Holy Spirit,

that those baptized in this water
may die to sin,
be raised with Christ,
and be born to new life in the family of your Church . . .

The Affirmation of Faith begins (8) with the candidates and/or the parent(s) (and godparent[s]) stating, in response to questions, that, by the grace of God, they turn away from evil and turn to God. In some liturgies, these questions and answers are known as 'The Decision'. The words that appear in *The Methodist Worship Book* are a truncated version of an ancient text, first used in the Eastern Church. Various forms of this text were developed over the following centuries, and most baptismal liturgies have it in some form. British Methodist services, however, did not include it until 1991.

The Affirmation (9) continues as all present say the Apostles' Creed, in three sections, each in response to a question asked by the minister. This Creed developed in the early Church in the context of Baptism and its earliest form consisted of three questions and three answers. The use of the Apostles' Creed in this interrogatory way in *The Methodist Worship Book*, and in many other contemporary liturgies, thus revives an ancient practice.

The minister now asks each candidate to say his or her name and/or asks the parent(s) of each child what name has been given to the child (10), and receives a suitable reply (11). The act of naming, something similar to which occurred, though only in the Infant Baptism service, in *The Methodist Service Book*, was not included in the draft edition of *The Methodist Worship Book*, but was added by the Revision Committee. The Faith and Order Committee had not included anything of this nature because of the widespread, but mistaken, belief that Baptism is essentially a naming ceremony. Though naming has sometimes appeared in

baptismal liturgies, it has always been intended to play a subsidiary part. The Revision Committee, however, supported a
proposed amendment to include this act of naming.

There may follow a few lines addressed by the minister to
those to be baptized (12). The history of this address is complex,
but the version which appears in *The Methodist Worship Book*
is based on the text included in *Uniting in Worship* (1988), the
service book of the Uniting Church in Australia. The alterations
were made to enable its use with both adults and children,
whereas the Australian version and its antecedents were suitable
only for infants. The address is a powerful proclamation of prevenient grace and an assertion that Christ's saving work was and
is for everyone.

Baptism is now administered (13, 14), the rubrics making clear
how this should be done. Water is poured over each baptizand's
head, or the baptizand is dipped in water, three times, once at the
mention of each Person of the Holy Trinity, as the traditional
Trinitarian words are said. When that has been done, the
minister declares that by Baptism, God has received the newly-
baptized person into the Church.

The sign of the cross is now made on the forehead of each
newly-baptized person, with suitable words accompanying this
action. This is another very ancient practice, though the place in
the service at which the signing occurs varies from liturgy to
liturgy and indeed there are precedents for more than one signing
during the service. Signing immediately after Baptism follows the
tradition of *The Book of Common Prayer* (1662), though
Common Worship (2000) places it after the Decision and before
the Prayer over the Water. The latter practice has the advantage
of clearly separating the signing from the Baptism in water, and
thus avoiding any confusion between the two, but the theological appropriateness of signing before Baptism, despite many
precedents, is open to question.

The traditional act of signing may be followed by the presentation of a lighted candle to each newly-baptized person, or, in the
case of infants, to the parent(s) or godparent(s) (15). This
medieval practice was not adopted by *The Book of Common*

Prayer or books influenced by it but was revived during the twentieth century, and introduced to British Methodism in 1975.

It sometimes happens that customs develop in local churches
and become widespread, before service books take any account
of them. An example of this is the practice of carrying newly-
baptized young children round the church to be shown to the
congregation, which was adopted in many churches even though
there was no suggestion of it in *The Methodist Service Book*. It
was decided to incorporate this action (16) into *The Methodist
Worship Book*, but also to make provision for those 'able to
answer', who are newly baptized, to stand facing the people,
who then say or sing the Aaronic Blessing ('The Lord bless you
and keep you . . .'). This, of course, is a most ancient blessing,
derived from the words of Aaron, recorded in Numbers 6.24–26.
It was not associated with Baptism in liturgies influenced by *The
Book of Common Prayer* (1662), though the proposals for that
book's revision in 1928 used it as a general blessing at the end
of the Baptism service. Its first Methodist appearance, as a
blessing addressed to the newly baptized, was in *The Book of
Offices* (1936); it was retained in 1975 and again in 1991 and
1999.

Up to this point, the four baptismal services have included
identical or very similar material, but, as the table on pp. 62f.
above shows, certain elements now start to appear in some
services, but not in others. (The section numbers given below
continue to be references to the first service.) The three services in
which young children feature include at this point the promises
of parent(s) (17) (and godparent[s]) (18) and the promise of the
people (19). The service for the Baptism of young children then
moves immediately to the (optional) presentation of a Bible
or some other book and of a baptismal certificate, a final prayer
and the Lord's Prayer (if the latter is not to be said later in the
service).

The service for the Baptism of young children, with Confirmation and Reception into Membership (of those baptized on a previous occasion), includes three elements (a Declaration, a Collect
and the opportunity for testimony) that do not need to appear, or

have already featured in, the other services. All three services in
which both Baptism and Confirmation take place now proceed
to a request for Confirmation (20).

The candidates kneel (21), and the minister, extending her or
his hands towards them, prays that they may be strengthened for
discipleship and filled with the Holy Spirit. The description of the
Spirit in this prayer is based on Isaiah 11.2, the citation of which
in this context is at least as old as the eighth-century Gelasian
Sacramentary. Then (22) the minister lays his or her hand on
each candidate's head, saying:

> Lord, confirm your servant N by your Holy Spirit that *she/he*
> may continue yours for ever.

It is unfortunate that this action and its accompanying words are
given a separate number from the preceding lines, for in truth the
Confirmation prayer is a unity. Most of it (21) is said only once,
but the last sentence (22) is repeated as many times as there are
candidates. There are parallels in this structure with the prayers
of Ordination, which will be discussed in Chapter Eleven. The
significance of the laying on of hands is considered at the end of
the present chapter.

The Introduction to 'Entry into the Church' offers only a very
brief account of the theology of Confirmation, so it may be helpful to quote from a 1992 report to the Methodist Conference
which adds a little more:

> The origins of Confirmation lie in the rite of Baptism itself,
> from which, in the West, Confirmation became detached in the
> early Middle Ages. The traditional understanding of Con-
> firmation among Christians of the Roman, Anglican and
> Lutheran communions, reflected in previous Methodist writ-
> ing on the subject, identifies two major elements in the rite. On
> the one hand, the Church prays that God will confirm (that is,
> strengthen) his servants for lifelong service. On the other hand,
> the candidates themselves confirm their membership of the
> Church, conferred by Baptism, and it has been characteristic

of some Methodist thinking to see Confirmation as a means of marking ritually the experience of coming to personal faith. To these important elements we might add a third: the concept of the Church as a confirming community, surrounding the candidates with prayer and love, and affirming their place within the corporate fellowship. But the emphasis should always be on God's confirming work: 'Lord, confirm your servant N by your Holy Spirit, that he/she may continue to be yours for ever.' First and foremost, it is God who confirms.

This emphasis on the confirming work of God is very clear in the current services, as is the close relationship between Baptism and Confirmation.

The act of Confirmation is immediately followed by Reception into Membership (23). These are distinct events. Confirmation is an act of the universal Church; Reception into Membership is very much a denominational matter. The latter reflects the origins of Methodism as a society, or series of societies, within the Church of England. As the words spoken to those being received make plain, reception is into the membership both of the Methodist Church and of the local church. This is important. Those now confirmed are not simply being received into a local 'society'; they become members of the whole Methodist Church. On the other hand, their membership is 'earthed'; it is recorded by the local church, which will provide pastoral care and nurture.

The Church Council will already have given its approval to the candidates' reception, and it is appropriate that a representative of the local church should join the minister in welcoming those who have been received as members (24).

Those newly confirmed and received now make three promises (25), relating to worship and service, daily discipleship and Christian witness. The congregation promises to maintain the Church's life of worship and service so that those newly (baptized and) confirmed 'may grow in grace and in the knowledge and love of God . . .' Gifts and certificates may be given (27). Each initiation service effectively concludes with a prayer (28) said by the whole congregation; and, in the case of all the services which include Confirmation, Holy Communion follows. 'Holy Communion for the Day of Pentecost and Times of Renewal in the Life of the Church' is the recommended order (30), though it would be right to use the appropriate seasonal order outside Ordinary Seasons.

Confirmation and Reception into Membership

Most of the ingredients of this service (pp. 97–102) have already been discussed above, since Confirmation and Reception take place in three of the four services which also include Baptism. In the account which follows, attention is drawn only to those places where there are differences from the other services.

The Declaration (2) briefly expounds the relationship between Baptism and Confirmation; it is a slightly amended form of a text first produced for the 1991 alternative service of Confirmation. The Declaration is followed by a short prayer (3) which links Baptism with the sustaining and strengthening work of the Holy Spirit.

The introduction to the Request for Confirmation (4) is subtly different from that in the other services (compare, for example, no. 20, p. 71), in recognition of the fact that, in this service, Confirmation is taking place some considerable time after Baptism, rather than a few minutes later! For the same reason, the final prayer (16) is an amended version of the prayer in the equivalent place in the services of Baptism.

The Laying on of Hands

There are several services in *The Methodist Worship Book* where hands are laid upon a person. This action is extremely ancient, and its precise significance varies according to its context, which is always made plain by the prayer which accompanies the act. This has been the case from biblical times. In Genesis 48, for example, the laying on of hands forms part of Jacob's blessing of

Ephraim and Manasseh; in Mark 6.5 it accompanies healing; and in Acts 8.17, it is associated with the reception of the Holy Spirit after Baptism. Setting apart, maybe even ordination, is the context for this sign in Acts 13.2f. and 1 Timothy 4.13.

Thus the action, always accompanied by prayer, is found in *The Methodist Worship Book* in the context of blessing ('A Celebration of Christian Renewal'), of healing ('An Order of Service for Healing and Wholeness'), of absolution ('A Service of Repentance and Reconciliation'), of prayer for the confirming (strengthening) work of the Holy Spirit ('Entry into the Church'), and of ordination ('Ordination Services').

8

Holy Communion

One of the most interesting features of *The Methodist Worship Book* is its generous provision of services of Holy Communion. As we have already noted, many people had been asking for more eucharistic material than had been supplied by *The Methodist Service Book* and the seven draft orders (plus an outline) issued in 1992 for trial use and comment were welcomed by most correspondents.

The Liturgical Sub-Committee was particularly interested in the enthusiasm shown by those correspondents for the provision of separate services for the major seasons of the Christian year. This innovative approach to the provision of several services had occurred to Group One of the Liturgical Sub-Committee at a very early stage as a way of achieving two very desirable objectives. First, it would enable the unique character of each season to be fully reflected in worship. Second, it would move away from the concept of a single service, containing a considerable number of options, including perhaps four or more eucharistic prayers. The latter method of supplying a variety of texts inevitably leads to much turning of pages and often also to confusion.

In this chapter, we shall consider various features common to all the services of Holy Communion, before considering particular elements in the individual services.

First, the basic elements of each service are indicated in *The Methodist Worship Book* by asterisks. These are such significant ingredients of a service of Holy Communion that they should in no circumstances be omitted (though Note 1, p. 115, stops short of saying that).

Second, the basic elements are combined in each service in an almost identical structure. The Lord's Prayer, however, appears after the prayers of intercession in some services and after the Great Prayer of Thanksgiving in others; this is indicated by brackets in the list below, which includes the basic elements and also those other elements which may be used in all, or almost all, the services. (The list does not apply to 'Holy Communion for Ash Wednesday' or to 'Holy Communion in a Home or Hospital'.)

THE GATHERING OF THE PEOPLE OF GOD

* Sentences
  Hymn
  Prayer of Approach/Adoration and/or Commandments
  (except in the Second Service during Ordinary Seasons)
* Prayer of Confession and Declaration of Forgiveness (not
  asterisked in Christmas, Easter and Pentecost)
* Collect
  Hymn or Canticle (asterisked in the Easter service)

THE MINISTRY OF THE WORD

* Either two or three readings from Scripture, the last of which
  is the Gospel
* Sermon
  Hymn
* Prayers of Intercession
* (The Lord's Prayer)
  The Peace (asterisked in the Easter service)

THE LORD'S SUPPER

The Preparation of the Gifts
  Hymn
* The taking of the bread and wine

The Thanksgiving
* The Great Prayer of Thanksgiving
* (The Lord's Prayer)

The Breaking of the Bread
* Bread is broken in the sight of the people
* Silence

The Sharing of the Bread and Wine
   Invitation to communion
* Bread and wine are received, with appropriate words said during the distribution
   There may be music during the distribution (not in the Lent Service)
* Remaining elements are covered

PRAYERS AND DISMISSAL

   Silence (asterisked in the Easter service)
   Prayer
   Hymn
   Blessing
* Dismissal

This structure, which is very much like that already familiar to Methodists from 'The Sunday Service', allows progression from the initial approach to God, through the reading and preaching of the Scriptures, to response through prayer and the celebration of the Lord's Supper.

   The Ministry of the Word in every service of Holy Communion contains certain basic elements: two or three readings from Scripture, the last of which is the Gospel, a sermon, and prayers of intercession. Other elements, such as a Psalm and hymns, may also be included. Sometimes the Peace is placed in this section of the service, though in other services the Peace is the opening act of the Lord's Supper. There is ancient precedent for both positions. On occasion, a Creed or another Affirmation of Faith is included in the Ministry of the Word.

The shape of the Lord's Supper deserves special mention. At the Last Supper, Jesus did seven things in relation to bread and wine:

1 Jesus took bread.
2 He gave thanks.
3 He broke the bread.
4 He gave it to his disciples.
5 Jesus took wine.
6 He gave thanks.
7 He gave the wine to his disciples.

The Church's liturgy reflects these actions, combining them together and thus reducing them from seven to four:

Jesus took bread and wine. (1 and 5 above)
He gave thanks. (2 and 6)
He broke the bread. (3)
He gave bread and wine to his disciples. (4 and 7)

The very shape of the service re-enacts this fourfold pattern. The four sections of the Lord's Supper are the Preparation of the Gifts, the Thanksgiving, the Breaking of the Bread and the Sharing of the Bread and Wine. Each one corresponds with one of the actions in the fourfold shape. So, when we celebrate the Lord's Supper, we not only recall what Jesus said and did; we also do similar things ourselves. The presiding minister takes bread and wine, leads the Great Prayer of Thanksgiving, breaks the bread, and presides over the distribution of bread and wine.

A third common feature of the services is that they contain a mixture of traditional texts and new compositions. The traditional texts include the Commandments of the Lord Jesus, canticles such as 'Glory to God in the highest', the Nicene Creed (which occurs in some, but not all, of the services), and the opening sentences of the Great Prayer of Thanksgiving and the *Sanctus* ('Holy, holy, holy Lord'), which are contained in every service. Otherwise, apart from a few texts borrowed from other sources (which will be noted below), all the prayers were composed for *The Methodist Worship Book*.

Fourth, every Great Prayer of Thanksgiving includes those ingredients which have traditionally been included in such prayers, though not necessarily in the same order. Each begins with the ancient dialogue, 'The Lord be with you. **And also with you**', followed by *Sursum Corda* ('Lift up your hearts . . .'), a feature of eucharistic prayers since at least the early third century, when they can be found in the *Apostolic Tradition* of Hippolytus. It would probably surprise many worshippers if they were told that, in participating in this dialogue, they are using words that have been common currency in eucharistic worship for at least 1,800 years. What a sense of the continuity of faith and worship, and of the communion of saints, can come from that knowledge!

The next section of the Great Prayer is always the Preface, an expression of thanks and praise for the mighty acts of God in creation and redemption. This is usually followed by the *Sanctus* ('Holy, holy, holy Lord . . .') and the *Benedictus qui venit* ('Blessèd is he who comes in the name of the Lord . . .') though, in a couple of the services, these words are included within the Preface. These texts have been associated with the Eucharist since the fourth century and possibly much earlier. Other elements of the Great Prayer of Thanksgiving – the order in which they appear can vary – are the Words of Institution, the Acclamation, an *Anamnesis*, an *Epiclesis*, Oblation, and a Doxology.

In the Words of Institution, the words and actions of Jesus at the Last Supper are recounted. The Acclamation is a shout of praise: a familiar example is 'Christ has died. Christ is risen. Christ will come again.'

Anamnesis is a Greek word which means 'remembrance'. Jesus told us to 'do this in remembrance' of him, and in every eucharistic prayer we state in some way that we are doing so: 'Remembering, therefore, his death and resurrection and proclaiming his eternal sacrifice . . .', and 'In obedience to his command we recall his suffering and death, his resurrection and ascension . . .' are two examples. As we have already observed, we remember him, not just in words, but by re-enacting in the service itself his actions at the Last Supper.

The *epiclesis* is that part of the eucharistic prayer in which there is invocation of the Holy Spirit. For reasons that will be explained later, every Great Prayer of Thanksgiving in *The Methodist Worship Book* contains the following *epiclesis*: 'Send [or "Pour out"] your Holy Spirit that these gifts of bread and wine may be for us the body and blood of Christ.'

In the words of Oblation the worshippers offer themselves in the service of God and ask to be united with Christ and with all God's people on earth and in heaven. Finally, every Great Prayer concludes with a Doxology, an ascription of glory and praise to God, Father, Son and Holy Spirit.

As was mentioned above, the *epiclesis* is an example of consistency within the Great Prayers of Thanksgiving. Church history provides evidence of a number of controversies about the eucharistic *epiclesis*. Such controversies have not really featured in Methodism, though one of the casualties of the consultation exercise was an *epiclesis* asking God through the Spirit 'to infuse this bread and wine with life and power', a deliberate echo of Charles Wesley's hymn, 'Come, Holy Ghost, thine influence shed' (*Hymns & Psalms* 602), with its lines 'Thy life infuse into the bread, thy power into the wine.' A number of correspondents found this Wesleyan-style *epiclesis* theologically unacceptable. It was wrong, they claimed, to ask for the Spirit to be poured out on inanimate objects. In the end, the Faith and Order Committee resolved to use in every Great Prayer the form of *epiclesis* suggested by the consultants who were appointed to review the comments on the 1992 draft services and make recommendations. This standard *epiclesis* is a deliberately ambiguous sentence which does not preclude our believing what Charles Wesley believed but does not absolutely require that we should. It could be taken to be no stronger than the essentially 'receptionist' sentence of 1975, which can only just be described as an *epiclesis*:

Grant that by the power of the Holy Spirit
we who receive your gifts of bread and wine
may share in the body and blood of Christ.

But it is capable of meaning much more. Theological ambiguity at this point is not disreputable, for in reality only God knows what happens, and it would have been wrong to include in a eucharistic prayer an unambiguous phrase which could cause unnecessary offence. But most members of the Liturgical Sub-Committee, and maybe others, will long regret the loss of Wesley's 'infusion'.

Whereas there is a standard form of *epiclesis*, the wording of the Words of Institution offers an example of deliberate inconsistency. Though the Institution Narrative is a traditional feature of eucharistic prayers, there is no universally agreed form, no one 'common text'. It has never been customary to quote directly or exclusively from any one of the biblical accounts (Matthew 26.26–29; Mark 14.22–25; Luke 22.14–20; 1 Corinthians 11.23–26), though they are the sources from which the narrative is ultimately drawn. It is as though Words of Institution have had a life of their own, independent of their sources. The Liturgical Sub-Committee took the view that there was no reason to reproduce the same version in every Great Prayer of Thanksgiving. For one thing, those who had drafted the individual services had come up with different versions, all of which had merit. For another, variant forms of the Words of Institution allow different ways of 'leading into' them (compare, for example, pp. 154 and 170).

Another common feature in this section of *The Methodist Worship Book* is the provision, in the opening section of each service, of a collect which may be used instead of the collect of the day, with the further possibility of some other prayer being said at this point. As a rule, it is better to say the collect of the day, but the inclusion of a printed prayer here means that this part of the service should not be passed over completely, as might have happened in some churches if there had been no more than a rubric relating to the collect of the day.

Throughout the service of Holy Communion, reference is made to the 'presiding minister'. Precisely what is meant by presiding at the Lord's Supper was a matter of some controversy during the 1980s, but Note 2 (p. 115) makes clear not only who may be a 'presiding minister' but also what his or her unique responsibilities are. As to the former, all Methodists who preside at the Eucharist are either ordained ministers (presbyters) or other persons authorized by the Conference to preside. Such authorizations are granted in circumstances where it can be shown that eucharistic deprivation would otherwise exist. As to the presiding minister's responsibilities, Note 2 explains that, although other people may be invited to share in other parts of the service, there are some words which should be spoken and certain actions which should be performed only by the person presiding at the service.

Finally, it is worth noting the rubric which is used, almost invariably, throughout *The Methodist Worship Book* in connection with the reception of the elements. Its first appearance is on p. 127 (25). There is a variety of practice within Methodism, as in some other churches, about this matter. The normative pattern throughout the Christian Church is for the presiding minister to be the first to receive the bread and wine, followed by those who are assisting in the distribution, and then by the people. It is probably true to say that the Liturgical Sub-Committee would have liked to rubricate for this practice without equivocation. But, recognizing that in some churches it is usual for people to receive in a different order, the Sub-Committee concluded that it would be wiser to hint at the traditional order, but without including words such as 'then', and to add the phrase 'according to local custom'. The only exceptions to the use of this rubric are in 'The Marriage Service' and 'The Blessing of a Marriage Previously Solemnized' (pp. 382 and 396), where provision is made for the husband and wife and their families to receive after the presiding minister and before the rest of the congregation.

Having considered all these matters which are relevant to 'Holy Communion' as a whole, we now turn to consider the individual services.

Holy Communion for Advent

The preparation of the Advent service was a difficult assignment because Advent has come to have a dual character. It is widely regarded as a time of preparation for Christmas; for many years lectionary readings (and themes, which *The Methodist Service Book* supplied) have accustomed worshippers to reflecting on the prophets, John the Baptist, Mary, and all who watched and waited and prepared the way for the coming of Jesus at Bethlehem. But Advent is also (and this is its more ancient focus) a penitential season when particular attention is paid to 'the Last Things' – Christ's coming in glory, and judgement. The Advent liturgy in *The Methodist Worship Book* emphasizes the latter, while aiming not to lose sight of the former.

The opening sentences (1) immediately set the tone with a reference (based on Luke 13.29) to the feast in the kingdom of God. A short prayer of adoration and invocation (3) recalls the prophetic tradition. The Commandments of the Lord Jesus (4) are included only in this service and in 'Holy Communion for Lent and Passiontide', being especially suitable for seasons of self-examination and penitence. The liturgical use of Christ's summary of the Law of Israel, in either its Matthean or its Markan version (it is the latter which appears in *The Methodist Worship Book*), can be traced back to the Non-Jurors of the early eighteenth century, but the inclusion of the 'New Commandment' (John 13.34) is a distinctively Methodist custom, dating from *The Book of Offices* (1936).

The prayer of confession and the declaration of forgiveness (5) are clearly appropriate for the season ('We have . . . ignored the message of those you sent. We are unprepared for the coming of your Son'; 'I am making all things new').

After the collect of the day, or the printed alternative (6), the collect of the Advent season may be said. The latter is a slightly revised version of a collect written by Thomas Cranmer for *The Book of Common Prayer* (1549); in the 1662 edition of that book it is stated that this collect 'is to be repeated every day, with the other collects in Advent, until Christmas Eve'.

One of two canticles or a hymn may follow. The canticles are obvious choices, both being songs from Luke's pre-birth narratives. *Benedictus* (see pp. 43f. above) is the Song of Zechariah, the father of John the Baptist; *Magnificat* (see p. 45 above) is the Song of Mary. In view of the association of the former with Morning Prayer and the latter with Evening Prayer, it would be most natural also to use the canticles in this way at Holy Communion as well during Advent, though *The Methodist Worship Book* gives no direction or suggestion to this effect. As in 'Prayer in the Morning', 'heaven' has accidentally replaced 'on high' in line 20 of *Benedictus*.

The Ministry of the Word follows, according to the pattern described on p. 74 above. There are two noteworthy features of the Ministry of the Word in this service. First, the prayers of intercession (15) are offered in the context of an expectation of Christ's coming in glory, as King, Lord, Judge and Saviour. Thus our future hope informs our present intercession. These prayers, as printed in *The Methodist Worship Book*, are borrowed, though in an amended form, from *The Promise of his Glory* (1990, 1991), prepared by the Church of England's Liturgical Commission.

The second interesting feature is the inclusion of the Prayer of Humble Access (17). The two versions of this prayer have been discussed in Chapter Three. We need, however, to pause at this point to consider the character of the prayer, the services in which it is included, and the question of the place in the service at which it should be said, if that is to happen.

As its name suggests, this prayer expresses the worshippers' sense of unworthiness to come to the Lord's Table and their utter dependence upon his mercy. First written by Thomas Cranmer for the 1549 Prayer Book, the prayer is dearly loved by many Methodists. The consultation exercise revealed widespread dismay that it had not been included as an option in every Communion Service; and a Memorial to the 1996 Conference asked that it should be so included. The 1997 Conference, however, adopted a report from the Faith and Order Committee that included these words:

Recognizing that the Prayer of Humble Access is very precious to many Methodists, the Committee proposes to include this prayer as an option in four services – Advent, Lent and Passiontide and two of the three 'Ordinary Seasons' services. This will make the Prayer of Humble Access available as an option on 42 of the 52 Sundays of the year. The optional material that has been provided in each draft service has been included on the basis that it is thought suitable for inclusion, if desired, in that particular service. In the Committee's judgement, the Prayer of Humble Access is well suited to the penitential seasons of Lent and Advent, and is not inappropriate during 'Ordinary Seasons'. It is not, however, well suited to the seasons of Easter and Christmas, nor to the Feast of Pentecost.

In the end, the Prayer of Humble Access was included five times in *The Methodist Worship Book*: in the services for Advent, Lent and Passiontide, one of the three 'Ordinary Seasons' services, 'Holy Communion in a Home or Hospital', and 'Extended Communion'. As the Faith and Order Committee's report suggests, the rather grovelling character of the prayer, appropriate enough during penitential seasons, is not well fitted to the great joyful festivals.

If the Prayer of Humble Access is to be included, where should it be placed? The traditional position for it is immediately before the minister and people receive the elements. The disadvantage of its inclusion at that point, however, is that it interrupts the fourfold shape which we considered earlier, preventing the reception of bread and wine from immediately following the Breaking of the Bread. 'Holy Communion for Advent' deals with this problem by placing the prayer earlier in the service, as a sort of transitional act which, together with the Peace, brings to an end the Ministry of the Word and leads into the Lord's Supper.

The Peace (18), if it is to be included, is introduced by an appropriate seasonal sentence. As in most of the Communion Services, the responsive sentences of the Peace may be followed by the people greeting one another in the name of Christ. The

Peace was not a feature of Western liturgies which followed the tradition of *The Book of Common Prayer* (1662), but was introduced to British Methodism in 1975 and to other then-contemporary liturgies, under the influence of *The Book of Common Worship of the Church of South India* (1967). It is a liturgical expression of the New Testament injunction to 'greet one another with a holy kiss' (see, for example, Romans 16.16; 1 Corinthians 16.20; 1 Peter 5.14). Most Methodist churches would already have established a pattern of including, or not including, the physical exchange of the Peace, prior to the publication of *The Methodist Worship Book*.

The Lord's Supper now follows, according to the pattern described earlier in this chapter. Readers who wish to do so will be able to identify the various features of the Great Prayer of Thanksgiving (21). The Preface moves from creation (by God's 'living Word'), through the message of the prophets and the preparation of 'the way for our redemption' to the incarnation. This is especially appropriate to Advent's role as a time of preparation for Christmas. The Acclamation, on the other hand, reflects the older Advent theme:

> . . . Christ will come in glory . . .
> He is Alpha and Omega,
> the beginning and the end;
> the King of kings, and Lord of lords.

The blessing and dismissal (32, 33) at the end of the service also give expression to the Church's future hope: 'The day of the Lord is surely coming . . .'

Holy Communion for Christmas and Epiphany

Like those who drafted the Advent service, the writers of 'Holy Communion for Christmas and Epiphany' needed to keep more than one theme in mind. This service is designed to be used from midnight on Christmas Eve until the Sunday after Epiphany. Traditional Christmas themes – the birth of Christ, the theology of the incarnation, the shepherds in the field – and traditional Epiphany themes – the visit of the Magi, the baptism of Christ – occur within this period.

Clearly some of the material in the service is more suited to certain occasions than others. The Invitation (3), for example, is particularly suitable for the midnight service on Christmas Eve, but would be less appropriate at an all-age service on the Sunday after Epiphany:

> In the silence and stillness
> let us open our hearts and lives to God,
> that we may be prepared for his coming
> as Light and Word, as Bread and Wine.

The confession and declaration of forgiveness (4) and the printed collect (5) have a seasonal feel to them, including as they do quotations from John 1. Although *The Methodist Worship Book* does not make this explicit, the fact that the confession and declaration are not preceded by an asterisk implies that it will not always be appropriate to include them. There is a case to be made for omitting confession on the great, joyful days of the Christian year, especially Christmas Day and Easter Day, each of which immediately follows a penitential season. The Feasts of the Epiphany and of Pentecost are also appropriate times to refrain from confession. The emphasis on these occasions should be on celebration, on rejoicing in God's mighty acts.

There is a choice between two canticles (6). 'Glory to God in the highest' is a hymn, dating from the fourth century, which was first used as an office canticle but became associated with the Eucharist early in the sixth century. At first it was used only on festal occasions, though it soon formed an invariable part of eucharistic worship on Sundays in the Western Church. In *The Methodist Worship Book* it is included in some, but not all, of the services of Holy Communion. The opening words of 'Glory to God in the highest' are derived from the angels' song in Luke 2, and the canticle thus has special significance at this time of year.

The alternative canticle, 'A Song of the Incarnation', which first appeared in *Hymns & Psalms* (1983), is an amalgam of verses drawn from the Old and New Testaments. It could be said at any time during the period for which this service is provided, but it seems most appropriate for the Feast of the Epiphany and the days immediately following it.

The prayers of intercession (14) are among the most remarkable in the book. Each of the four main sections consists of three parts, the first of which is always a statement about Christ's coming. In the opening section, for example, the text reads:

Unlooked for,
Christ comes.

To shepherds,
watching their sheep through the long, dark night,
he comes with the glory of the angels' song
and the humility of the manger.

Prayer then follows, initially in silence, and then in words which take up themes from the statement. So, for instance, in the opening section the themes of human life and work, represented by the shepherds, and the glory and humility of God's love, are woven together in the prayer:

Loving God, we pray for our community . . . In the midst of our everyday lives, surprise us with glimpses of the glorious, humble love at the heart of existence.

Each section ends with the versicle and response:

Lord, come to your people.
In your mercy set us free.

The four sections include prayers for the community, the leaders of the nations, the Church, and those in need. These are linked to the stories of the shepherds, of the wise men, of Anna and Simeon, and of Christ's baptism, respectively. The coming of the wise men and the baptism of Christ are 'Epiphany' themes, and one of the remarkable qualities of these intercessions is their appropriateness at any service throughout the period from Christmas Eve to the Sunday after Epiphany.

The next feature of this service that deserves special mention is the prayer (20) said when the presiding minister takes the bread and wine and prepares them for use. In only three of the services of Holy Communion are words allocated to this part of the service. In 'Holy Communion for Christmas and Epiphany' and in 'Holy Communion for Ordinary Seasons (First Service)' the same prayer appears at this point, whereas 'Holy Communion for the Easter Season' has a series of liturgical exclamations, rather than a prayer.

The Liturgical Sub-Committee was aware that care must be taken to ensure that any words which accompany the Preparation of the Gifts should not anticipate the offering of the eucharistic elements which will take place during the Great Prayer of Thanksgiving. (Not all compilers of service books have been so scrupulous.) The beautiful prayer which is provided links the bringing of bread and wine with the offering of the worshippers' lives and gifts (which may be, though need not be, monetary gifts) and looks forward to their transformation through God's grace and love.

As might be expected, the Preface in the Great Prayer (21) and the sentences at the breaking of the bread (22) have an emphasis appropriate to the seasons for which this service was prepared. The post-communion prayer (29) is a very slightly amended form of an equivalent prayer from *The Alternative Service Book* (1980). Where *The Alternative Service Book* and *The Methodist Worship Book* refer to 'the hope that you have set before us', the original version of this prayer, published in the Anglican 'Series 3' service in 1971, read 'the hope that we have grasped'. The amended text is certainly an improvement: first, because 'grasped' is a rather ugly word and second, because it is theologically preferable to regard hope as something 'set before us' by God rather than as something which we ourselves have 'grasped'.

Although the Acknowledgements omit to say so, the blessing (31) is an amended version of the blessing written by Eric Milner-White for inclusion in the service of Nine Lessons and Carols at King's College Chapel, Cambridge.

Holy Communion for Ash Wednesday (or for the First Sunday in Lent)

Ash Wednesday is the first day of Lent and, since a service of 'Holy Communion for Lent and Passiontide' is also provided in *The Methodist Worship Book*, it may be wondered why a separate service is needed for this day. In fact, 'Holy Communion for Ash Wednesday' is not a complete order of service; it may be regarded as a version of 'Holy Communion for Lent and Passiontide', 'customized' for Ash Wednesday; and those using it have to turn to that service before the prayers of intercession. It would have been possible to incorporate the Ash Wednesday material into the full Lent service, but this would have involved many options and page-turnings, which the chosen method of dealing with Ash Wednesday has avoided. The comments which follow concern only those elements unique to the Ash Wednesday service.

Note 1 (p. 141) indicates that, where it is not possible to use this service on Ash Wednesday, it may be used on the following Sunday.

The address (3) briefly describes the history and emphases of the season of Lent and invites the worshippers to observe the season appropriately. This address has been borrowed, with acknowledgement though not without amendment, from the Episcopal Church of the United States of America. Indeed, as we shall see, the whole service is enriched by texts from America, Canada and New Zealand. The printed collect (5) can be traced back to the earliest version (1549) of *The Book of Common Prayer*, for which it was composed by Cranmer. In the Prayer Book tradition, this collect was read after the collect of the day throughout Lent, and a similar suggestion is made in *The*

Methodist Worship Book (p. 534), though there is no reference to this in 'Holy Communion for Lent and Passiontide'. In view of the provision of a rubric about the collect for Advent, the omission of something similar in the Lent service seems strange. It was almost certainly an unintentional omission.

In the Ministry of the Word, verses from the penitential Psalm 51 are set out in full. On this occasion, the translation is not *The New Revised Standard Version*, but comes from *A New Zealand Prayer Book* (1989), with one minor amendment in the second line. The Ten Commandments (12) make their only appearance in *The Methodist Worship Book* after the sermon, grouped together in two sections with a versicle and response after each section.

There follows an act of penitence, which begins with a silence (13) and continues with a prayer of confession (14) and a further silence (15) before an optional ashing ceremony (16) and a declaration of forgiveness (17). The omission of an asterisk before the prayer of confession is almost certainly an oversight, since the silences on either side of it have asterisks and such a prayer should not be omitted during this penitential season. The prayer comes from a Canadian source, *The Book of Alternative Services* (1985), where it appears in a rather longer form.

If there is to be an ashing ceremony, a prayer is said and the sign of the cross is applied in ash to the forehead of the presiding minister and of everyone who wishes to receive this sign. The words which accompany the signing make clear that it is a reminder of our human mortality and encourage us to turn from sin and be faithful to Christ.

Ashing ceremonies have become more common in Methodist churches than once they were, though it is probably true to say that only in a small minority of churches will this ceremony be found. Some correspondents suggested during the consultation process that ashing is in direct contravention of Matthew 6.16–18; though in fact what is condemned in those verses is the motive of those who publicly display their piety.

The power of signs and symbols will be discussed in Chapter Nine. It is perhaps sufficient at this stage to say that a ceremony of ashes, understood, as Note 2 (p. 141) suggests, as a sign of repentance and a symbol of mortality, can be a helpful ingredient of an Ash Wednesday service; but, where it is not deemed appropriate, the service can perfectly well proceed without it. Even when it happens, it is optional for members of the congregation. Note 3 (p. 141) gives some practical information and advice about ashing.

After the declaration of forgiveness (17), the Ash Wednesday service continues from the intercessions in 'Holy Communion for Lent and Passiontide'.

Holy Communion for Lent and Passiontide

After the opening sentence (1) and a hymn (2), the Commandments of the Lord Jesus, which we discussed on p. 80 above, may be said. The prayers of confession which follow (4) are marked with an asterisk; this is the only service in which that is the case, but it would be unthinkable to omit confession during the penitential season of Lent. In recognition of the fact that the focus of the season changes from the Fifth Sunday in Lent onwards, when Passiontide begins and the mystery of Holy Week and Easter draws closer, two collects are printed (5), one for the period up to the Fifth Sunday and the other for use thereafter.

A hymn or the canticle 'Saviour of the World' (6) may follow. This canticle is unusual in two ways. First, it is relatively modern, having been composed in the nineteenth century. Second, it was written from within the Free Church tradition, almost certainly by Henry Allon, a Congregationalist minister. It was clearly inspired by the medieval antiphon 'O Saviour of the world, who by thy cross and precious blood hast redeemed us, save us and help us, we humbly beseech thee, O Lord'.

The next feature of the service which we stop to consider is the Affirmation of Faith (13), which takes the form of the Apostles' Creed. This is unusual in eucharistic services in which, if a Creed is included, it is normally the Nicene Creed, the Apostles' Creed being more closely associated with initiation services.

The Apostles' Creed is used in this service as a faint echo of the practice of the early Church, whereby 'catechumens' (those being prepared for Baptism) were taught the Creed during Lent, prior to their Baptism at Easter.

The prayers of intercession (15) are shorter than in some of the other eucharistic liturgies, though their form encourages, indeed almost requires, the insertion of words about specific topics or people at the places indicated by dots.

The Peace (16) is introduced by an appropriate seasonal sentence, but there is no suggestion (as there is in every other Communion Service in *The Methodist Worship Book*) that the people may greet one another. The omission is quite deliberate. While at other times of the year, even in Advent, it may be desirable for this sign of Christian fellowship to be shared among the congregation, it is more fitting, during the solemn and penitential Lenten days, to refrain from it. The greeting will be all the more welcome and meaningful when it happens again during the exuberantly joyful season of Easter.

The *Sanctus* comes earlier in the Great Prayer of Thanksgiving than in most of the other services – just over halfway through the Preface. There is no strong reason for this, though it does follow one ancient tradition (others place the *Sanctus* later).

Interesting rubrics and text appear at the Breaking of the Bread (21), where, in addition to performing that action, with optional words, the presiding minister may also lift the communion cup, with or without words. A careful reading of the rubrics indicates that, while the first action is basic to the service, the second is not. After all, the worshipping community is re-enacting what Jesus did in the Upper Room, and lifting the cup was not one of his seven recorded actions, whereas breaking the bread was. So the lifting of the cup is optional. Its inclusion in this service (and in 'Holy Communion during Ordinary Seasons, Second Service' and 'Third Service') alongside the Breaking of the Bread is without significant liturgical precedent at this point in the service, but some people may find its visual impact helpful. (In *The Book of Common Prayer* [1662] and many services indebted to it, rubrics direct that the bread be broken and the cup taken into the priest's hand during the 'Prayer of Consecration'.)

Agnus Dei, 'Lamb of God' (23), now makes its first appearance in *The Methodist Worship Book*, though it will appear in further services. 'Lamb of God', which is based on John 1.29, 36 and the middle section of 'Glory to God in the highest', was, from the late seventh century, an anthem sung at the Breaking of the Bread (and, at a later period, during communion). There are several English versions of 'Lamb of God'; the one included at this point in *The Methodist Worship Book* is from *Praying Together* (1988), prepared by the English Language Liturgical Consultation, although the Acknowledgements (p. 602) overlook the fact. The omission was reported to the 2001 Conference and in future editions of *The Methodist Worship Book* a new paragraph will appear, correcting that mistake as well as those in the texts of *Benedictus* and *Te Deum Laudamus* (see p. 44 above).

The Prayer of Humble Access (24), which we discussed extensively on pp. 81f. above, is here placed in its traditional position, immediately before the Sharing of the Bread and Wine. This prayer and 'Lamb of God' are both options, and it is not desirable to include both of them, though there is no indication of that here, as there is in 'Holy Communion during Ordinary Seasons (First Service)' (p. 195).

The second set of words of invitation (25) is a shortened and amended version of an invitation from John Hunter's *Devotional Services* (1890). If the Prayer of Humble Access has been said, it may be better for the first form of invitation to be issued, since the second invitation covers much the same sort of ground as the prayer.

The post-communion prayer (29) is based on a text from the fifth-century Liturgy of Malabar. *Hymns & Psalms* 626 is derived from the same source.

Holy Communion for the Easter Season (including Ascensiontide)

After the self-examination and penitence that characterize Lent and Passiontide, it is appropriate, during the great Fifty Days of Easter, to sound the note of joy and thanksgiving. 'Holy Communion for the Easter Season' differs in many ways from the previous service, not least in its overall mood.

Like 'Holy Communion for Lent and Passiontide', however, the Easter service recognizes that a shift takes place during the season itself. Easter is the celebration of Christ's resurrection, but as Ascension Day approaches, so the focus turns towards the events of that day and, during the period from Ascension Day to Pentecost, there needs to be more emphasis on Christ's exaltation and eternal reign. In a number of places, therefore, more than one text is supplied, in order to acknowledge the developing themes of the season. The opening sentences (1) illustrate this point.

The prayer of adoration (2) is Trinitarian in structure and content and focuses on the theme of life. It may be followed by a prayer of confession (3). Penitence is a note which should have been clearly sounded during Lent; it is appropriate to have rather less penitence and much more rejoicing during the richly contrasting season of Easter. Especially on Easter Day, confession is best omitted altogether. But there are 50 days of Easter and the short, direct prayer of confession which is provided sets penitence in the context of Christ's victory.

Two other options as well as 'Glory to God in the highest' (6) and a hymn are suggested. The first is 'A Song of Resurrection', known as 'The Easter Anthems' in *The Book of Common Prayer* (1662). It is a collection of verses from Paul's letters to the Corinthians and the Romans, which, in a shorter form, was used in traditional monastic offices during Eastertide and in the late-medieval Sarum rite was sung during a procession at the Eucharist on Easter Day. 'A Song of Christ's Glory' is made up entirely of verses from Philippians 2, thought by some scholars to be an early Christian hymn, quoted rather than composed by Paul.

The word 'Alleluia' quite properly appears in many Easter hymns and other liturgical texts, and, in this service alone, is inserted in the words (11) which precede and follow the Gospel. This is one way in which the service stresses the distinctiveness of Easter, the 'Queen of Seasons'.

The prayers of intercession (14) have a clearly defined structure. First, God is asked to 'remember . . . in . . . love the Church throughout the world . . .' Silence follows. Then there is a one-sentence prayer for the Church, followed by a versicle and response, which link the themes of love and life:

Lord of life,
hear us in your love.

This pattern is reproduced as God is asked to remember the world, those who suffer and those who have died.

'Alleluia' is also included in the words spoken at the Peace (17). This is one of only two services in which the Peace is marked by an asterisk. The Liturgical Sub-Committee judged that it was appropriate to regard the Peace as a 'basic element' of the service during the Easter season, because John's account (John 20.19–31) of the risen Christ's appearances in the Upper Room three times includes the words 'Peace be with you'. For the Peace not to be exchanged, at least verbally, during the Easter Season would therefore be strange.

The Preface in the Great Prayer of Thanksgiving (20) is punctuated by an ascription of glory, said twice by the congregation:

Blessing and honour and glory and power,
are rightly yours, all-gracious God.

It is as though the congregation's Easter jubilation is such that the worshippers cannot refrain from interrupting the presiding minister and bursting in with their joyful shout of praise!

The first set of sentences at the Breaking of the Bread (21) is the opening words of 'A Song of Resurrection'. The second set is in its present form as a result of a discussion in the Liturgical Sub-

Committee about an equivalent text in *The Methodist Service Book*, which reads:

> The things of God for God's holy people.
> **Jesus Christ is holy, Jesus Christ is Lord**
> **to the glory of God the Father.**

The first sentence is a variant of a text which can be traced back to many ancient eucharistic liturgies, originating in the East as early as the fourth century: 'holy things for holy people'. The second sentence, spoken by the congregation, is in part a quotation from Philippians 2.11, where it is said that every tongue will confess that Jesus Christ is Lord, to the glory of God the Father. In the Liturgical Sub-Committee, it was argued that, as they stand, the words printed in bold type do not make sense, for surely, in Philippians, it is the confession of Christ's lordship which is to the glory of God. The liturgical sentence suggests that Christ's holiness and lordship are to the glory of God, which is a possible, though unlikely, interpretation of Philippians.

The matter was resolved by making the congregational response into a joyful acclamation:

> **Jesus Christ is holy;**
> **Jesus Christ is Lord.**
> **Glory to God the Father.**

For the post-communion prayer (28) and for the blessing (30) two texts are offered, the second in each case being especially appropriate for Ascensiontide. The service ends, as it began, with the word 'Alleluia!'

Holy Communion for the Day of Pentecost and Times of Renewal in the Life of the Church

Contrary to a widespread misconception, there is no such thing as a season of Pentecost. The Day of Pentecost brings to an end, not only the Easter season, but also the first part of the Christian year which started on the First Sunday of Advent. After the Day of Pentecost and until Advent comes around again, it is Ordinary Time.

There is only one day, therefore, in the Calendar for which this service is specifically designed, but it may also be used at what are described as 'times of renewal in the life of the Church'. Examples of such times of renewal are suggested at various points in *The Methodist Worship Book*, for instance on pp. 342, 364 and 518.

Not surprisingly, on the day when the Church commemorates the empowerment of the apostles by the Holy Spirit, there is more emphasis in this service than in any other on the person and work of the Spirit. The tone is set immediately in the opening sentence (1) and the prayer of invocation (3) and continued in the prayer of confession and declaration of forgiveness (4) and the printed collect (5). An early draft of the confession included the words 'your Spirit is light', which were changed as soon as their ambiguity was spotted! The original inspiration for the confession, though the text has been altered almost beyond recognition, is a prayer from the *Book of Divine Services* (1984) of the Presbyterian Church in Cameroon.

The prayers of intercession (14) are another example of the indebtedness of *The Methodist Worship Book* to service books of other churches, both in Britain and overseas. In this case, the prayers are based on intercessions from *A Book of Services* (1980), published by the United Reformed Church.

The Preface in the Great Prayer of Thanksgiving (19) is strongly Trinitarian, but with greater emphasis than in most eucharistic prayers on the work of the Holy Spirit. The sentence before the final doxology brings together the themes of unity and mission which have featured earlier in the prayer.

Two sets of sentences (21) are provided at the Breaking of the Bread. The first is the opening words of the 'Easter Anthems', because Pentecost is not simply a special day in its own right, commemorating the coming of the Spirit upon the apostles; it is also the fiftieth and final day of the Easter Season.

The post-communion prayer (28) asks God to transform, lead and equip those present, through the character and gifts of the Spirit, for worship and service. The blessing (30) is extremely unusual in reversing the order of the Persons of the Trinity ('Spirit, Son and Father'), reflecting the order in which the three Persons are mentioned in the introduction to the blessing.

Holy Communion during Ordinary Seasons (First Service)

Three services are provided for 'Ordinary Seasons', the definition of which is given in the Note (p. 185). It was the intention that each of the three services should have a different 'feel'. The first was designed to be easily accessible to people accustomed to 'The Sunday Service' (1975), and in general it follows a similar pattern. It includes the Collect for Purity (3), which all previous Methodist service books have included, in the tradition of *The Book of Common Prayer*. Its first-known appearance was in an eleventh-century missal, but it has been attributed to St Gregory, an eighth-century abbot of Canterbury. In the Sarum rite it was part of the priest's private devotions before the service, and in *The Book of Common Prayer* (1662) and other services in the Prayer Book tradition, including Methodist services, it was said by the minister alone. This custom survived into *The Methodist Service Book* (1975).

The prayer of confession (4) is based on a text produced by the Joint Liturgical Group, an ecumenical body set up in the 1960s which, from its inception, has included representatives of the Methodist Church. It was the Joint Liturgical Group which produced the Lectionary included in *The Methodist Service Book* and the one which was authorized for use in Methodism from 1991 to 1998. More will be said about these lectionaries in Chapter Eighteen.

The intercessions (14) are brief and direct, though there is space, as usual, for the mention of particular people and concerns. The Nicene Creed (17) is printed here, as well as in the Second Service. It was felt that it would sometimes, though not invariably, be desirable for the Creed to be said during Ordinary Seasons.

The prayer 'Lord and Giver of every good thing' (20) appears here and in the service for Christmas and Epiphany; it has been discussed on p. 86 above.

The Great Prayer of Thanksgiving (21) is unique in the book in providing 'proper prefaces', words designed for one specific day or occasion. These are not generally needed, because there are five seasonal services. But two great occasions, Trinity Sunday and All Saints' Day, seemed to cry out for special recognition. It would have been excessive to have produced complete services for these days, important though they are, but special words are supplied for them, which follow the general Preface and precede the *Sanctus*. The text for Trinity Sunday comes from *The Alternative Service Book* (1980) and that for All Saints' Day from the South African book *An Anglican Prayer Book* (1989).

'The Sunday Service' (1975) offered three sets of sentences at the Breaking of the Bread. Versions of the first two are carried forward (22) into the service which we are presently considering. In the first, the Liturgical Sub-Committee has substituted 'in one bread' in the congregational response for the widely disliked phrase from 'The Sunday Service', 'in the one loaf'. The second set begins with a version of the ancient 'holy things for holy people', different from that which we have noted in the service for the Easter Season:

The gifts of God for the people of God.

The response is a joyful exclamation:

May Jesus Christ be praised!

which will be suggestive, to many worshippers, of a hymn (*Hymns & Psalms* 276) which repeatedly uses these words.

The silence (23) which follows the Breaking of the Bread may lead into the saying of one of four printed texts (24). 24A is 'Lamb of God' (see above, p. 91); 24B is a text based, like 'Lamb of God', on John 1.29, but supplemented by allusions to Revelation 19.9 and Matthew 8.8; and 24C and 24D are two versions of the Prayer of Humble Access. This section is not marked with an asterisk, however, so a fifth possibility is that the silence will lead directly into the Sharing of the Bread and Wine (25).

The post-communion prayer (30) is deliberately carried over from 'The Sunday Service', for which it was written. It was a prayer which many people had come to know by heart and to love, and it seemed right to include it in at least one service in *The Methodist Worship Book*. For obvious reasons, the prayer has been amended by the substitution of 'people' for 'mankind'.

The printing of two verses of a hymn (31) revives an older Methodist tradition. There are few good things to be said about the Second Order for Holy Communion in *The Book of Offices* (1936), which was designed to offer an accessible way in to those Methodists who, prior to Methodist Union, had not been familiar with 'liturgical services' in the Prayer Book tradition. The one stroke of genius in that service, however, was the inclusion of two verses of Charles Wesley's great Easter hymn 'Christ the Lord is risen today' after communion. They were not included in 'The Sunday Service', but have made a welcome reappearance in *The Methodist Worship Book*. It has been said that 'every Sunday is a little Easter'; in other words, Sunday is the Day of Resurrection and every Sunday Christ's people celebrate his risen presence. It is entirely appropriate, whenever this service is being used, for the verses to be sung, though another hymn may be used (or none at all).

Another link with 'The Sunday Service' lies in the fact that the blessing (32) and the dismissal (33) are virtually identical to those in the older service.

Holy Communion during Ordinary Seasons (Second Service)

When a draft version of this service was issued for trial use, it was described as being particularly suitable for use at all-age worship. It was produced with such services in mind, and, though a decision was made not to draw attention to the fact in the final version, the language and content suggest that, of the three services for use during Ordinary Seasons, this will generally be the one most suitable when people of all ages are present.

The most distinctive feature of this service is its provision of musical settings at various points. Note 2 (p. 198) makes clear that these settings are examples only; other versions may be used, and will surely be needed if the service is used on a regular basis.

Apart from the traditional texts, for example 'Glory to God in the highest' (5B) and the Nicene Creed (12A), the hymns and other musical settings, and the Affirmation of Faith (12B), the words of this service are entirely new.

The prayer of confession (3) draws a contrast between God's love and call to human beings and the human response. Divine love is emphasized in the declaration of forgiveness and the printed collect (4), which is richly Trinitarian, asks, among other things, that we may be helped to love and serve God.

A hymn or 'Glory to God in the highest' or some other act of praise (5) may follow. The sung version of 'Glory to God' (5A), sometimes known as the 'Peruvian Gloria', requires a leader. Only a melody line is available until the last two bars when some harmony is supplied; this canticle is best sung unaccompanied. Unaccompanied singing is also possible with the other musical settings, though, with a little research, organists and pianists will be able to find full music versions, if accompaniment is desired.

An Affirmation of Faith (12B) is offered as an alternative to the Nicene Creed. Like the interrogatory form of the Apostles' Creed, which was discussed in Chapter Seven, this Affirmation reflects the origins of that Creed in the practice of the early Church, when those being baptized were asked three questions about belief, one in respect of each Person of the Holy Trinity. This particular Affirmation is an amended form of a text which appeared in *The Alternative Service Book* (1980). The latter was itself indebted to a question in the Catechism included in *The Book of Common Prayer* (1662).

Unusually, no text is supplied for the prayers of intercession (13), though the topics which they should cover are clearly set out.

The Great Prayer of Thanksgiving (17) is the location of the controversial phrase 'God our Father and our Mother', which has been discussed in the Introduction and in Chapters One and Two. The prayer is punctuated at intervals by singing and its language is particularly straightforward and direct.

This is one of those services where the act of breaking the bread may be accompanied by the lifting of the cup (19). The post-communion prayer (27) is loosely based on the opening verses of 1 John.

Holy Communion during Ordinary Seasons (Third Service)

The third service begins with 'The Grace' (1). These words (from 2 Corinthians 13.13) are often regarded as suitable closing words, but only in 'An Order for the Blessing of a Home', which is obviously a domestic service rather than an act of public worship, and in 'A Vigil' (see p. 168 below) does *The Methodist Worship Book* use the Grace in this way. Words of blessing and dismissal are more fitting at the end of an act of corporate worship; the Grace is better used as a greeting at the start of a service.

A prayer of approach (3) is followed by confession (4), first in silence and then in a series of sentences, followed by a form of *Kyrie eleison*. The canticle 'You are Worthy' (6) now makes its only appearance in *The Methodist Worship Book*. It is a collection of verses from Revelation 4 and 5, first employed as a canticle in the early twentieth century. A number of different translations have been used in recent service books; the one which appears in *The Methodist Worship Book* was specially prepared for it.

Another distinctive feature of this service is the provision (13) for a time of quiet reflection or testimony after the sermon. This is one of the ways in which *The Methodist Worship Book* suggests possibilities which those responsible for planning services might not otherwise consider.

The prayers of intercession (15), after a Trinitarian introduction, address God in terms of some of the divine attributes ('God of love, . . . of mercy, . . . of compassion, . . . of glory') and in turn offer prayer for the Church, the world and those who suffer, and remember the faithful departed. As usual, there is the opportunity for more detailed concerns to be expressed.

The Great Prayer of Thanksgiving (19) allows for slightly more active congregational participation than is customary; in addition to the usual places where the congregation joins in the prayer, there are two invocations, to Jesus and the Holy Spirit, before and during the *epiclesis*.

Guidance for Ordering a Service of Holy Communion

The two pages of Guidance were very late inclusions in *The Methodist Worship Book*; they were inserted at the Revision Committee stage. Like the similar material in the section 'Morning, Afternoon, or Evening Services', these notes are designed to assist leaders of worship whose congregations will not have in their hands copies of *The Methodist Worship Book* or any other printed liturgy. The ingredients that should, or in some cases simply may, be included in a service of Holy Communion are listed, and there is a particularly detailed description of the content of the Great Prayer of Thanksgiving.

Holy Communion in a Home or Hospital

Ministers are often asked to lead services of Holy Communion in private homes, nursing homes, hospitals and hospices, for those not able to attend worship in their local churches. This short service is designed for that purpose. It frequently echoes the 1936 service from *The Book of Offices*, a lineal descendant of the service of Holy Communion from *The Book of Common Prayer* (1662). Older people in particular will find phrases which resonate with them, not least in the Collect for Purity (2), the prayer of confession (3), the Great Prayer of Thanksgiving (10) and the Prayer of Humble Access (13).

Extended Communion

The copious Notes (p. 229) accompanying this service carefully distinguish it from the preceding service, which is a full service of Holy Communion. 'Extended Communion', however, is, as its name suggests, an extension of a service that has already taken place. Bread and wine, previously set apart at a service of Holy Communion, are taken by a presbyter or a deacon, or by an authorized lay person, to those unable to attend the celebration in church, in order that they may receive the bread and wine and so share in the community's celebration.

This is a very ancient practice, described in what is one of the earliest surviving accounts of Holy Communion, that of Justin Martyr in the middle of the second century. The practice was commended to Methodism in a report from the Faith and Order Committee in 1984, and again in 1994 and 1996. The 1995 Conference adopted a service of 'Extended Communion', on which the liturgy in *The Methodist Worship Book* is closely modelled.

The declaration (3) is borrowed from *Ministry to the Sick*, a Church of England publication which dates from 1983. The Collect for Purity (4) and the prayer of confession (5) are identical to those in 'Holy Communion in a Home or Hospital'. Because of what has already happened in the church service, there is no taking of the bread and wine, no Great Prayer of Thanksgiving, and no Breaking of the Bread. These have already occurred. A short general thanksgiving (9), however, appropriately precedes prayers of intercession.

This service brings to a close the longest section of *The Methodist Worship Book*. Never before has the Methodist Church had such abundant provision for its eucharistic worship.

9

Holy Week Services

One of the most fascinating documents to have come down to us from the early Church is the *Itinerarium Egeriae* (or 'Egeria's Pilgrimage'). Dating from the late fourth century, it describes a three-year pilgrimage round the Holy Places undertaken by Egeria, a member of a religious community from Gaul or Spain. Her account of the Holy Week ceremonies in Jerusalem is of particular interest. At that time, these ceremonies were unique to that city: the sanctuaries that had been built in places associated with the events of Holy Week lent themselves to vivid and powerful re-enactments of those events in the very places where they were believed to have occurred. No doubt as a result of the reports carried back to their homes by Egeria and by many other pilgrims to Jerusalem, the dramatic observance of Holy Week spread rapidly throughout the Christian world.

There is nothing in earlier Methodist service books, however, that corresponds with 'Holy Week Services'. Though these services stand in a long tradition, that tradition, for the most part, has bypassed British Methodism. In recent years, however, many Methodists, by sharing in Local Ecumenical Partnerships or participating in ecumenical services, have come to experience and appreciate the rich opportunities which Holy Week presents for us 'to identify and be united with Christ in his sufferings so that we may share his risen life' (as the Introduction, p. 235, puts it.)

Signs and Symbols

'Holy Week Services' is the section of *The Methodist Worship Book* in which the widest range of visual symbols and symbolic actions appears. Many of these will be unfamiliar to many Methodists, who are only slowly coming to appreciate the value of signs and symbols. Within living memory, opposition could be encountered to a proposal to have a cross prominently on display in a church. Candles were virtually unknown. Places of worship tended to be plainly, even austerely, furnished. There was little to appeal to the eye, or indeed to any sense other than that of hearing, during acts of worship. The only exceptions were the use of water at Baptism and of bread and wine at Holy Communion.

The Methodist Service Book (1975) allowed for relatively little symbolism, other than those material things which are essential to the two sacraments. A lighted candle could be presented at infant Baptism, though this option was not taken up in many places for some time. Rings were, of course, exchanged in marriage services, though God was asked to bless the giving of the rings, rather than the rings themselves. It may be that ecumenical contact has influenced Methodism in the matter of symbols and symbolic actions, or that the search for alternative forms of worship has had an impact, but it is certainly true that there is now a greater use of the visual, for example in the form of banners and candles.

Compared with its predecessor, *The Methodist Worship Book* has a much stronger sense of the power of signs and symbols. Candles may be given to the baptized, whatever their age, and *The Methodist Worship Book* does not shrink from asking God to bless the rings themselves at a wedding (see Chapter Thirteen). There is also the opportunity for ashing at the start of Lent, for foot-washing on Maundy Thursday, not to mention the stripping of the communion table later that day, for the lighting of an Easter Candle at the Easter Vigil and subsequently at Baptisms, for the laying on of hands and/or anointing with oil at a Service for Healing and Wholeness, and for the blessing of domestic buildings as well as the dedication of church buildings and their furnishings.

Underlying all this is a theological principle. Christianity is an incarnational religion, which declares that in Christ God's Word became flesh. The purely spiritual was revealed in tangible form. Christianity is also a sacramental religion, in which it is believed that God uses material things to convey grace. It may be that *The Methodist Worship Book* will enable Methodism to experience more fully the power of signs and symbols and to discover the ways in which worship can be enriched by them.

Palm Sunday

As the Introduction (p. 236) explains, worship on Palm Sunday should have two distinct elements. The first is a recognition of Palm Sunday as an important day in its own right, on which it is proper to recall and celebrate Christ's entry into Jerusalem. The second is a looking forward through the coming Holy Week to the Cross, since it is traditional for the whole of one of the Synoptic Gospel Passion Narratives (Matthew 26.14—27.66; Mark 14.1—15.47; Luke 22.14—23.56) to be read on this day.

The use of symbolic objects (palm branches or palm crosses) and a symbolic action (a procession) is encouraged in the Notes (p. 236). Ideally, the congregation will gather away from the church building and then go in procession to it, though a procession can be held within the building itself.

Appropriate responsive sentences (1) are followed by an invitation to the congregation to go with Christ on his entry into Jerusalem and all that it will entail. The prayer which may be said over the palms (2) asks that they may be for those carrying them a sign of Christ's victory. The story of Christ's entry into Jerusalem is read from one of the Gospels (3) and the singing of 'All glory, laud, and honour', or some other hymn, may accompany the procession. 'All glory, laud and honour' came into widespread use almost immediately after its composition by St

Theodulph of Orleans around AD 820. The original text had 78 lines, some of them rather quaint.

After the procession, one of the collects for Palm Sunday or some other prayer is said (5), and the service continues from the Ministry of the Word. If the Passion Gospel is read in full, it is appropriate for the sermon to be shortened or even omitted. Most worshippers are not accustomed to hearing extended readings from the Bible, and a complete Passion Narrative can speak very powerfully for itself without the need for any exposition. It is possible to buy books in which the Passion Gospels are set out to be read by more than one person; in some versions, there is a narrator, a voice speaking the words of Jesus, and another who takes all other speaking parts. A long reading of this sort is certainly more likely to come to life if there is more than one reader.

No form of service is provided for the next three days of Holy Week, though the Lectionary suggests readings for them. In most Methodist churches, the next liturgical acts are likely to occur on Maundy Thursday.

Maundy Thursday

Maundy Thursday was the day on which Jesus instituted the Lord's Supper and it is fitting that Holy Communion should be celebrated on this day. It would have been possible for the Maundy Thursday service to have been included in the 'Holy Communion' section of *The Methodist Worship Book*, but it seemed better not to detach it from the other Holy Week services, or from the other liturgical acts which may follow Holy Communion on Maundy Thursday.

The service begins (1) with the words 'On this night . . .', words which will be repeated several times during the service. The opening sentence quotes the words from which the term 'Maundy' is derived (the Latin *mandatum* means 'commandment').

The prayer of confession (3) is 'borrowed', with alterations, from the Church of England's *Lent, Holy Week, Easter* (1984,

1986). It is more than usually expansive, as befits a day in Holy Week, although the principal emphasis during a Maundy Thursday Communion Service should be on joy and thanksgiving for Christ's gift of this sacrament. A joyful note is sounded if 'Glory to God in the highest' (4) is said or sung, probably making its first appearance for many weeks.

After the sermon (11), there may be foot-washing, about which guidance is given in Note 2 (p. 240). Some people find this re-enactment of Jesus' act of humble service profoundly moving and challenging. Others feel that, in a society where it is not commonplace for guests' feet to be washed on their arrival at a host's house, this symbolic act is alien and embarrassing. It is an option within the service.

The prayers of intercession (15) skilfully weave together events that occurred 'on this night . . .' with prayers for the church and for the needy. They are derived, again in an amended form, from *Lent, Holy Week, Easter.*

'On this night . . .' appears yet again in the introduction to the Peace (17). Only in this service and in 'Holy Communion for the Easter Season' is the Peace marked with an asterisk. The Liturgical Sub-Committee decided to regard the Peace as a basic element in this service because the words of John 14.27 were spoken on the first Maundy Thursday, and because the Last Supper was a sort of 'proto-Eucharist'.

The Preface in the Great Prayer of Thanksgiving (21) aptly makes mention of the night of the Passover and God's feeding of his people in the wilderness. Although other eucharistic prayers refer to 'the night' in which Jesus was betrayed, this prayer is uniquely able to refer to it as 'this night'.

Unusually, a hymn (26) is printed in full for possible use during the distribution. This thirteenth-century hymn by St Thomas Aquinas is believed to have been written for the feast day Corpus Christi (a festival devoted to the institution of the Eucharist) and it is thus at least as appropriate on Maundy Thursday. The translation printed in *Hymns & Psalms* (624) has been modified by the omission of one verse and the amendment of another, in the interests of inclusive language.

The post-communion prayer (29) is one of the collects of the day. It may be followed by a hymn (30), after which there are a number of possibilities. If no further liturgical acts are to take place, some stark words, centred on Jesus' words in Gethsemane, are spoken, and the congregation leaves in silence. Such an ending to the service is in marked contrast to what usually happens immediately after a service and it helps to reinforce the sense of a change of mood. The joyful celebration of Christ's institution of the Lord's Supper is now over; Good Friday looms.

Provision is next made in *The Methodist Worship Book* for either 'The Gospel of the Watch' or 'A Service of Light and Darkness', either of which may be the final liturgical act of the day, or may be followed by 'The Stripping of the Communion Table' or 'A Prayer Vigil' or both. Pages 252 and 253 consist almost entirely of rubrics, the preparation of which required a great deal of care.

'The Gospel of the Watch' (33–4) is a short act during which the story of Jesus in Gethsemane, Peter's denial, and perhaps (depending upon which Gospel is used) the trial of Jesus, is read from Matthew, Mark or Luke.

'A Service of Light and Darkness' (36–8) is longer. The greater part of the Passion Narrative from one of the Synoptic Gospels is divided into 16 sections (Matthew and Luke) or 14 sections (Mark), after the reading of each of which a candle is extinguished and a period of silence kept. The table on p. 254 indicates where the sections begin and end. Prayers and hymns may also be included. Apart from candlelight, which steadily diminishes as this service proceeds, there should be as little light as possible in the building.

'The Stripping of the Communion Table' (42) and the removal of other decorations from the church can be a powerful evocation of the coming desolation of Good Friday, whether done in silence or during the reading of Psalm 22.

'A Prayer Vigil' (44) envisages the possibility that the congregation may stay, perhaps for an extended period, to 'watch and pray', using prayers, readings and maybe other material to enable that process.

At whatever point the day's proceedings come to a close, all leave in silence.

Good Friday

The Notes (p. 255) encourage the minimal use of musical instruments and the provision of adequate time for silent prayer during worship on this most solemn of days. There are five occasions where a period of silence is rubricated, quite apart from the silences included in the prayers of intercession.

The collect (2) has been associated with Good Friday (or sometimes the Wednesday of Holy Week) since its inclusion in the eighth- or ninth-century Gregorian Sacramentary. The Old Testament reading (3), in which the prophet Isaiah of Babylon envisages the Suffering Servant of the Lord, has long been regarded by the Church as an evocative passage which, whoever the prophet's 'Servant' may have been, is suitably used in Christian devotional contemplation of the sufferings of Jesus Christ. Similarly, Psalm 22 (5), which, according to Matthew 27.46 and Mark 15.34, was quoted by Jesus on the Cross, is the obvious choice of Psalm for this solemn day.

There is a long tradition which reserves the reading of the Passion according to St John for Good Friday, and *The Methodist Worship Book* follows that tradition (9). As on Palm Sunday, it will be helpful if the Passion Gospel is read by more than one person.

There is a suggestion (12) that a wooden cross may be carried to the front of the church. This symbolic act may be followed by 'the Reproaches' (13), Scripture-based sentences put into the mouth of Christ, reproaching the human race for its ingratitude, and interspersed with the words of the *Trisagion* (see above, p. 51). The Reproaches were introduced into the Roman rite sometime in the eighth century (or possibly earlier), where they formed part of a ceremony known as the Veneration of the Cross. Although the rest of that ceremony is absent from *The Methodist Worship Book*, the inclusion of the Reproaches, a text quite unlike any other, is a welcome feature of this service. Their use can be astonishingly moving.

The canticle (15) is a collection of New Testament verses, interspersed with 'We praise and adore you, O Christ . . .' Like 'Saviour of the World' (see p. 89 above), the response was inspired by the medieval antiphon 'O Saviour of the world, who by thy cross and precious blood hast redeemed us, save us and help us, we humbly beseech thee, O Lord'.

The prayers of intercession (17), after a short introduction, have a threefold structure which is repeated several times. First, topics for prayer are mentioned, concluding with a versicle and response. Second, there is a time of silence. Third, the prayers are summed up in a collect. The first collect (p. 260) was one of the Solemn Prayers for Good Friday in the Gelasian Sacramentary. The second (p. 260) is also ancient; it is the Joint Liturgical Group's version of a prayer from the Roman Missal, which did not originally have an association with Good Friday. The third (p. 261), written by the Liturgical Sub-Committee, is discussed in Chapter Eighteen (see p. 205 below). The collect, 'God our redeemer' (pp. 261f.), was written by the Joint Liturgical Group. 'Gracious God, the comfort of all who sorrow . . .' (p. 262) is a version of a prayer which appeared in *The Book of Alternative Services* (1985). The final collect (p. 263) in these prayers of intercession was included in the provision for Good Friday in the Joint Liturgical Group's *Holy Week Services* (1983).

The service ends with prayer (20). One of two collects may be said; the first (20A) is also used in *The Methodist Worship Book* as the first collect for the Fifth Sunday in Lent and the second (20B) as the first collect for the Third Sunday in Lent. They are discussed in Chapter Eighteen (see pp. 202 and 201 below).

There is no dismissal or blessing. As on Maundy Thursday, all leave in silence.

The Easter Vigil

Accounts have come down to us from the early Church of vigils held on Holy Saturday, otherwise known as Easter Eve (Easter Saturday being the Saturday *after* Easter Day). The Introduction (p. 265) describes the features of these ancient vigils, from which this service takes its form.

The Easter Vigil takes place during the hours of darkness and has four principal sections:

The Vigil
The Service of Light
The Reaffirmation of Baptism
Holy Communion.

The Vigil begins with opening sentences (2) which indicate the characteristics of the service which is to follow – vigil, prayer and celebration. Next (3) follow at least three Old Testament readings, each of which is accompanied by a Psalm, a part of a Psalm, or a canticle, by a collect, and by a period of silence (to which, unfortunately, no reference is made in set A). A scriptural refrain is provided in each case, which may accompany the Psalm or canticle. In all, there could be nine sets of readings, Psalms, and so on, though this would almost certainly be too much for the average congregation, considering that much else is yet to happen.

The Old Testament readings invite meditation on the following themes: creation, the flood, Abraham's preparedness to sacrifice Isaac, the Exodus, God's sustenance of his people, Wisdom, and God's cleansing and restoration to life of his people, to whom new life and new hope are given. In the Psalms, canticles and collects which accompany them there is also much that is suggestive of Christian Baptism and of the resurrection hope.

The opening lines of collect A (p. 268) are reminiscent of an ancient collect (from the Leonine Sacramentary) which is used as the first collect for the First Sunday of Christmas. The second part, however, is developed differently, with attention focused not on Christ's incarnation, but on his sacrifice. There is a clear allusion to 1 Corinthians 5.7, which is the opening verse of the 'Easter Anthems' (see above, p. 92). Collect A has been published in a number of forms; the version given in *The Methodist Worship Book* exactly follows the South African text in *An Anglican Prayer Book* (1989).

Collect B (p. 268) is the work of the Liturgical Sub-Committee, though lines 2 to 4 are copied from 'the Prayer over the Water' in the 1991 *Entry into the Church* services. Collect C (p. 269) is adapted from *The Book of Alternative Services* (1985).

The Book of Common Worship of the Church of South India (1963) is the original source of collect D (pp. 269f.), though the text as printed here is substantially the same as that published by the Joint Liturgical Group in 1978. The Liturgical Sub-Committee amended two prayers composed by the International Commission for English in the Liturgy to produce collects E (p. 270) and F (p. 271).

Collect G (p. 271) is also used in *The Methodist Worship Book* as one of the collects for the Twenty-sixth Sunday in Ordinary Time. It is discussed in Chapter Eighteen.

Collect H is the collect for Holy Saturday; it dates from the Scottish Prayer Book of 1637. Collect I (p. 273) comes from the Australian book *Uniting in Worship* (1988).

A silent procession (5) to the entrance of the church marks a significant change of mood in 'The Easter Vigil' as the Service of Light begins. For this part of the service an Easter Candle is required, which may be prepared, as indicated in Note 5 (p. 266), during the service itself (6). Then the candle is lit, to the accompaniment of words (7) which make it clear that the candle represents the light of the risen Christ. This symbolism is reinforced as the person carrying the candle raises it (8) and says: 'Christ our Light' and the people respond: 'Thanks be to God.' The procession moves to the centre of the church (9) where the candle is again raised and the words are repeated, but this time more loudly. Now the candles of those who are assisting are lit from the Easter Candle (10), the procession moves to the front of the church and the words 'Christ our Light' are said yet more loudly. Only those who have experienced a procession of this nature know how powerfully evocative it can be.

The light is then spread more widely as the congregation's candles are lit (11). This is the time for the year's first joyful cry 'Alleluia! Christ is risen!', with the triumphant reply: '**He is risen indeed! Alleluia!**' Some people may find it strange that these words could be said at, say, 10 o'clock on Holy Saturday evening rather than being reserved until Easter Day, but the Jewish custom of regarding a day as beginning at sunset informed the Easter Vigil from the outset.

The note of celebration continues in the saying or singing of the *Exsultet* (12) in one of the two forms printed. This hymn is said to have originated in north Italy in the fifth century. The translations are from *The Roman Missal* (1975) and *Lent, Holy Week, Easter* (1984, 1986) respectively.

A most remarkable prayer of thanksgiving (13) follows, which in its present form is based on a prayer from the South African publication *An Anglican Prayer Book* (1989). It celebrates the events of this 'most blessed of all nights', linking them with the Passover, the crossing of the Red Sea, Baptism, paradise restored, and the reconciliation of all creation to God. Its imagery is powerful and vivid.

A rubric (14) like no other in *The Methodist Worship Book* indicates that 'a fanfare may be played, cymbals clashed, bells rung, lights switched on and the people's candles put out'. The last two actions are purely practical, but the putting into effect of any of the first three would, to say the least, be unusual in a Methodist Church. But that is no reason to ignore the rubric; Holy Saturday is no ordinary night.

'Glory to God in the highest' (15), which ought not to have been said during Lent (other than on Maundy Thursday), makes a welcome return. Then follows the collect of Easter Day (16), whose origins lie in a Holy Week collect from the eighth- or ninth-century Gregorian Sacramentary, but which has been progressively amended, especially during the twentieth century, to make it unequivocally appropriate for Easter.

In some traditions, the order of the Vigil and the Service of Light is reversed, and a rubric (17) makes provision for this to happen. It seems better, however, to spend the earlier part of the service in prayer, praise and meditation on themes largely suggested by the Old Testament, and then to move on, in the Service of Light, to a celebration of Christ's resurrection.

A pastiche of verses from the Psalms (18), accompanied by nine congregational repetitions of 'Alleluia', leads into what is effectively the Ministry of the Word, which includes Romans 6.3–11 (19), where St Paul powerfully links Baptism with Christ's death, burial and resurrection, and (21) a Synoptic Gospel account of Christ's resurrection.

The Reaffirmation of Baptism follows (24, 25). In some other branches of the Christian Church, something called 'The Renewal of Baptismal Vows' takes place at this point. Most Methodists, however, having been baptized in infancy, have never made baptismal vows, and so are unable to renew them. Their parent(s) and maybe godparent(s) or sponsor(s) will have made promises, accepting their own responsibility for the Christian upbringing of their children, but that is not at all the same thing. In those denominations where Renewal of Baptismal Vows does take place, vows (rather than promises) will have been made in services of infant Baptism and parent(s) and god-parent(s) will be deemed to have spoken for the child in making those vows.

This difference in theological understanding means that the emphasis in the Reaffirmation of Baptism is different from what it would be in a Renewal of Vows. In *The Methodist Worship Book*, the faith in which the people were baptized is reaffirmed by the corporate saying of the Baptismal (Apostles') Creed (24) and there is a prayer (25) which links Baptism with the worshippers' ongoing pilgrimage and with Christ's death and resurrection.

The service continues from the prayers of intercession in 'Holy Communion for the Easter Season'. The Nicene Creed is omitted, since the Apostles' Creed has been said.

These 'Holy Week Services' were carefully prepared with the

aim of introducing to British Methodism some of the liturgical treasures cherished by other parts of the universal Church. There is much in these pages that, by engaging senses other than that of hearing, can enrich worship and enable the sorrows and joys of this great week to find appropriate liturgical expression.

10

The Covenant Service

If there is one form of service that is generally regarded as distinctively Methodist, it is the Covenant Service, even though, as the Introduction (p. 281) emphasizes, early Methodist Covenant Services were hugely indebted to seventeenth-century Puritan writers. But it is true that, from the time of John Wesley onwards, Methodists have continued to hold this service annually, and for many it is a treasured part of their devotional life. In more recent years, Christians of other traditions have often come to value Covenant Services, either by attending them in Methodist churches, or by including material from the Covenant Service in their own liturgies.

Nevertheless, opinion is sharply divided among Methodists about this service. Some criticisms of it relate to language, especially that of parts of the Covenant Prayer, and these will be considered later. But others are concerned with the essential character of the service. Fully to participate in it requires a person to make a most significant act of commitment to God. Some people are content to do this, and find the challenge which the service annually presents to them helpful in their Christian lives. Others, however, believe that the service demands more than can reasonably be expected of the average Sunday-morning congregation, which may consist of a wide range of people, to some of whom the underlying concepts of the service may be both strange and forbidding. It has also been suggested that the service is too individualistic (the pronoun 'I' is used throughout the Covenant Prayer, for example) and no longer suitable as an act of corporate worship. The last criticism can to some extent be met by the observation that the Covenant Prayer is said by the whole congregation, and that, although it certainly implies individual commitment, that commitment is made in a corporate context. As the Introduction (pp. 281f.) says: 'The covenant is not just a one-to-one transaction between individuals and God, but the act of the whole faith community.' The Introduction (p. 282) also addresses the point about commitment: 'The service is meant to lead us, by a path both similar to and differing from that of normal Sunday worship, to that commitment which all worship seeks both to inspire and to strengthen.'

Before 1936, the style and content of Covenant Services were very different from what they have been since that date. Earlier forms contained a great deal of exhortation and relatively little prayer. The service in *The Book of Offices* (1936) introduced Methodists to a different style of Covenant Service, in which little (apart from the Covenant Prayer itself) was retained from earlier forms. The 1936 pattern was modified in 1975 and has been further modified by *The Methodist Worship Book*, but the present form of the service is clearly in the direct line of descent from 1936.

The Notes (p. 282) indicate, first, that the Covenant Service should normally be held only once a year and, second, that it should be regarded as the principal service of the day on which it is held and should be used in full. *The Methodist Service Book* made it plain that the Covenant Service should conclude with the Lord's Supper, but *The Methodist Worship Book* goes further by supplying material for the Lord's Supper which is unique to the Covenant Service. There is therefore no need for a congregation to find its way from one part of the book to another and, still more importantly, the Covenant Service is able to reflect its central theme from start to finish.

The prayers of adoration (2) are an improved version of equivalent prayers in the 1975 service, which themselves were a modification of the 1936 prayers. They are Trinitarian in shape and content. In the two previous Covenant Services, confession was included after adoration, but in the new service it has been deferred until after the Ministry of the Word. The collect (4) is a revision of a 1975 text.

Some unusual features of the Ministry of the Word deserve comment. First, it will be observed that four readings (5, 6, 7, 9) are prescribed, with the Old Testament providing two of them, one from the Law of Israel and one from the Prophetic tradition, as well as an Epistle and a Gospel. Since 'covenant' is so obviously a concept which is deeply rooted in the Old Testament, this makes a good deal of sense. Second, each of the first three readings has appropriate sentences for the reader and the congregation to say after it has been read. Usually sentences of this sort are said only after (and before) the Gospel. The Covenant Service's additional sentences help to draw attention to the different elements of the biblical tradition.

The section of the service which is called The Covenant begins (12) with a short exposition of the history and meaning of 'covenant'; this, again, is a revision of a 1975 passage. After it, the presiding minister invites the people to seek forgiveness, and the prayers of confession (13) follow.

The penitential prayers in *The Book of Offices* Covenant Service were long and detailed, and those who prepared *The Methodist Service Book* decided to include a much shorter act of confession. Rather to the surprise of the Faith and Order Committee at that time, and subsequently, there was a widespread feeling that this part of the service had been too drastically pruned. As a result, the Liturgical Sub-Committee resolved to strengthen the penitential section, as compared with 1975, while not going as far as the service of 1936.

Each section of confession is followed by the beautifully simple

Lord, have mercy,
Lord, forgive

which compares favourably with the 1975 sentence:

Have mercy on us, Lord, and forgive us.

Charles Wesley's best-known hymn on the Covenant is sung (14) and the service proceeds to the introduction to the Covenant Prayer (15) and the prayer itself. This part of the service takes one of two forms and, for reasons which will become apparent, the second form will be considered before the first.

The introduction and the prayer, as set out in 15B, are almost identical to the words which appeared in the equivalent place in *The Methodist Service Book*. These are the words that most life-long Methodists have always associated with the Covenant Service. But these words have not been without their critics. In particular, the words 'Put me to doing, put me to suffering' have caused concern and it has often been remarked that any words which need a footnote to explain them (as in 1975) should not appear in a liturgical text at all. On the other hand, the familiar words were precious to many people. Responding to several requests, the Liturgical Sub-Committee resolved to explore the possibility of a new version of the prayer, which would attempt to express the same concepts but would not simply 'translate' the well-known words. To the surprise of several members of the Sub-Committee, a remarkably promising first draft was pro-duced, and both the Sub-Committee and later the Faith and Order Committee devoted a good deal of time to refining it. It appears as 15A. Time will tell whether the 1999 Covenant Prayer will, like the 1975 Prayer of Humble Access, become the better-known version, deplored by some people but beloved by others. Whichever version of 15 is used, each participant is making a wholehearted commitment to accept the will of God and to serve as and where God chooses. It is entirely proper that all should be standing both for the introduction and for the prayer (this was not the case in the 1975 service where the people stood for the former but sat or knelt for the latter).

Silence (16) is a fitting conclusion to such a prayer. Inter-cession was entirely absent from the 1975 service, but is included in its successor (17) with another version of the prayer which appears on pp. 34–5, and which has been discussed in Chapter Six.

The Lord's Supper may begin with the Peace (18), introduced by a sentence which reflects a number of biblical texts, including Isaiah 55.3 and Ezekiel 37.26.

Perhaps surprisingly, the word 'covenant' appears only once

during the Great Prayer of Thanksgiving (21), and that occurs in the Words of Institution ('This is my blood of the new covenant'). But the Preface makes much of what is the basis of the Covenant: God's utter dependability, faithfulness and love, revealed in creation, in the Law and the Prophets, and supremely in Christ, the living Word. The sentences at the Breaking of the Bread are the same as the second set of sentences in 'Holy Communion for the Easter Season' and have been discussed in Chapter Eight.

   In the final prayer (30) God is thanked for nourishing the worshippers for their continuing pilgrimage, and an eschatological note is sounded in the reference to 'the feast of [God's] eternal kingdom'.

II

Ordination Services

When the draft edition of *The Methodist Worship Book* appeared, some people wondered why it contained 'Ordination Services', which would never be used in most churches, since nearly all Methodist ordinations take place at the time of the annual Conference, in locations close to the Conference venue. It was even suggested that valuable space could be saved by omitting the two Ordination Services from the main book, and publishing them separately, though clearly they would need to be authorized by the Conference.

Yet even with the 'minimalist' approach which informed *The Methodist Service Book*, the one Ordination Service required in 1975 was included in that book. The reason for that – and the reason for including Ordination Services in the successor volume – is that such services are not just forms of worship, but are also expressions of a Church's understanding of ordained ministry. It is important that they should be easily available for study and reflection, both by Methodists, browsing through the book at home or in church, and by Christians of other traditions, who wish to know what Methodists understand by ordination. The best way of achieving these ends is by publishing the Ordination Services in the Church's authorized worship book.

The Introduction (pp. 297f.) sets ordination in the context of the calling of all Christian people, the whole people of God, within which some people 'are called and ordained to specific ministries'. Then follows a useful, though necessarily brief, account of presbyteral and diaconal ministry in the Methodist Church, the manner in which ordination takes place, and the Church's intention in ordaining.

The Ordination of Presbyters, Usually Called Ministers

It is only relatively recently that the term 'presbyters' has been more than occasionally used in the Methodist Church, and the title of the service reflects this fact. In the official constitutional documents of the Methodist Church it is clear that the term 'minister' refers to a minister of the word and sacraments (that is, a presbyter). Since deacons are also ordained to a ministry, there is abundant scope for confusion, which could be avoided if 'presbyter' rather than 'minister' were to achieve more general usage. That time may come, but the Faith and Order Committee judged that it had not yet arrived and therefore that both the words 'minister' and 'presbyter' needed to be included in the title of this service.

The presiding minister at Ordination Services is the President of the Conference, or the President's deputy who is usually, though not invariably, a former President. In the two Ordination Services, and in this commentary, 'the President' means the presiding minister.

The service begins with a prescribed time of silence (1). This is unusual, but Ordination Services are always very well attended and there is often much animated conversation before the service. It is customary for some information and guidance to be given to the congregation five or ten minutes before the service is due to start, and, when this has been done, the congregation is asked to prepare for worship in silence. The ordinands and those who are to lead worship normally enter the church during this silence.

The President and the people then say the opening sentences (2), from Psalm 136.1, after which the President welcomes the people and says the Grace, the congregation responding appropriately. This is one of relatively few services in *The Methodist Worship Book* where specific hymns are recommended. 'The Saviour, when to heaven he rose' (*Hymns & Psalms* 211) has been sung at Methodist ordinations since 1936.

Like most of the other printed texts in this service, apart from 'common texts', the collect (4) is an original composition. It sets the tone for all that is to follow.

The Old Testament reading (5) recounts the call of the prophet Isaiah; it has been used in the presbyteral ordination service since 1936. The first 12 verses of the Epistle (6) were included in the *Ordinal* (1968) which was published in connection with the Anglican/Methodist Conversations of the time; these verses found their way from the *Ordinal* into *The Methodist Service Book* (1975). This passage is a splendidly appropriate appeal for dedication to God and for the exercise of gifts within the one body that is the Church.

Before the Gospel, Charles Wesley's great hymn of praise, 'Ye servants of God, your Master proclaim' (*Hymns & Psalms* 278), or some other hymn is sung (7). The Gospel (8) is St John's account of the risen Christ's appearances to his disciples in the Upper Room. It too was used in the services of 1968 and 1975.

After the sermon (9), the Nicene Creed is said, as is fitting on such a great occasion. The ordinands will later be questioned about their belief in the doctrines of the Christian faith, and it is right that that faith should be professed by all at the end of the Ministry of the Word.

A solemn moment is reached as the Secretary of the Conference (or a deputy) presents the candidates to the President (11). Each rises as his or her name is read by the Secretary. When all the candidates have risen, the people also stand (12) and the President asks them whether they believe that the candidates are, by God's grace, worthy to be ordained. The people respond, 'They are worthy.' This traditional ceremony, Orthodox in origin, in which the whole congregation assents to the ordination of candidates, is important, not only as an encouragement to the candidates, but also as an indication that ordination is the act of the whole Church. A further question elicits a promise from the congregation to uphold the candidates in their ministry. The inclusion of something similar in 1975 was influenced by the Anglican/Methodist *Ordinal* (1968).

Next comes the Examination (13), which falls into two sections. In the first, the President addresses the ordinands, indicating what their responsibilities and privileges as presbyters will be. This is the nearest thing to a 'job description' for presbyters that the Methodist Church has so far produced. It should be noted that, as well as listing the duties that will necessarily be carried out by individual ministers, acting alone – duties such as preaching, presiding at the Eucharist, and so on – the address hints at the 'collegial' nature of ordained ministry:

> These things are your common duty and delight. In them you are to watch over one another in love.

There is also a reminder that their ministries will make great demands on the ordinands and those close to them.

In the second part of the Examination (and this is really the Examination proper) the President asks the ordinands to declare their lifelong commitment to presbyteral ministry by answering five questions about their call, their acceptance of the Scriptures, their belief in the doctrines of the Church, their acceptance of the Church's discipline, and their intention to be faithful in worship, prayer and study.

In the litany (14), after a time of silence, prayer is offered for the world, the Church, those called to be ordained, those whom they serve, and those close to them. The structure of these petitions is rather unusual; in each case the indirect object is mentioned first (for example, 'On the people . . .'), followed by the subject ('Gracious God') and then the main verb and object of the sentence ('pour out your Spirit'). On paper, they look strange, yet they flow well enough in practice. These prayers conclude with the saying of the collect, 'Remember, O Lord . . .', which can be traced back as far as the Leonine Sacramentary. More information about this collect (the third collect for Ash Wednesday) is to be found on p. 200 below.

The hymn, *Veni Creator* (15), associated with Ordination Services since the eleventh century, is now sung, before the ordination prayer (16) is said. It is important that the nature of this prayer should be understood; both the Introduction (pp. 297–8) and the rubrics in the service itself are designed to make it clear that, though the prayer is in three parts, it is a single prayer. The first part is said only once; it is a thanksgiving for the succession of ministries, derived from Christ himself, which extends through the centuries to the present time. The second part of the prayer, said as many times as there are ordinands, is a petition for the Holy Spirit to be sent upon the ordinand for the office and work of a presbyter, and the saying of the words is each time accompanied by the laying on of hands. The final part of the prayer is said, once only, when hands have been laid on all the ordinands, petition being offered that God will fulfil in them the work he has begun.

Other ministers join the President in the laying on of hands. This is a traditional practice which symbolizes the collegial nature of presbyteral ministry. At one time, it was customary for a large number of ministers to lay on hands, but the Conference resolved in 1996 to amend Standing Orders so that the number of ministers joining in the laying on of hands is restricted to two.

An ancient tradition underlies the giving of a Bible to each newly-ordained presbyter (18). Known as the *porrectio instrumentorum*, it consists of the presentation of symbols of office. Though of course secondary to the act of ordination itself, in the form of prayer with the laying on of hands, the giving of the Bible is a significant moment in the service. For several years it has been customary for the Vice-President of the Conference or a deputy to make this presentation, even though *The Methodist Service Book* did not allow for this practice. It was suggested to the Conference during the 1980s by the Faith and Order Committee in response to requests for greater lay participation in the service.

Another solemn moment arrives as the President declares (19) that the new presbyters have been duly ordained and charges them to fulfil their ministry. Then comes an unusual rubric (20), 'The people may welcome the newly-ordained Ministers with applause.' It was suggested to the Revision Committee that this rubric be removed, but the Committee and the Conference judged that it should be retained. Once again, it reflected what had become a frequent practice at ordinations, though there was no formal provision for it in the 1975 service. Even some of those who would prefer it if there were no applause will agree that, if there is to be clapping, it is better for there to be some direction as to when this should occur. Applause in this context is best understood as a sign of rejoicing in the ordination that has just taken place, rather than as a sort of recognition of the achievements of those newly ordained.

The service now proceeds to the Lord's Supper, beginning with the Peace (21). It has its own Great Prayer of Thanksgiving (24) which, in an unobtrusive way, includes allusions to the Church's ministry and the ministry of presbyters which are clearly appropriate on such an occasion. At the end of what is always a long service, the section after communion is deliberately brief. The post-communion prayer (31) reflects the prayer from the Liturgy of Malabar, which was discussed on p. 91 above.

The Ordination of Deacons

No Ordination Service for deacons was included in *The Methodist Service Book* because in 1975 it was judged that the decision to ordain women, as well as men, to presbyteral ministry would result in the eventual disappearance of the Wesley Deaconess Order. Candidature for the Order had drastically declined and recruitment ceased entirely in 1978. But by 1986 it was becoming clear that people, male as well as female, were still hearing God's call to diaconal ministry, and procedures for candidature were once more made available. The Methodist Diaconal Order came into being and the Faith and Order Committee was directed to draw up an Ordination Service, which was authorized in 1989 and first used at the Conference of 1990.

In *The Methodist Worship Book*, an entirely new service for 'The Ordination of Deacons' appears, which, in its structure and some of its content, is closely akin to 'The Ordination of Presbyters'. The fact that the two services are so similar is important for two reasons. First, it makes clear that the two services, like the two orders of ministry, are of equal status. Second, where there are differences between the liturgies, these differences are necessary because the diaconal and presbyteral ministries are distinct, and the services help to elucidate where the distinctions lie.

So, for example, there is no need for the two liturgies to have different opening sentences (2), or litany (14), but different Bible readings (5, 6, 8) are appropriate and the Examination (13), the Ordination Prayer (16), and the Declaration (20) must also be worded differently from their equivalents in the service for presbyters. Close comparison of the equivalent sections of the two services is an instructive exercise.

One feature of 'The Ordination of Deacons' to which there is no parallel in the other Ordination Service is the presentation of the badge of the Methodist Diaconal Order (19) to each newly-ordained deacon. In Methodist understanding, deacons are members of a religious order as well as belonging to an order of ministry. This fact has also influenced the opening sentences of the Declaration (20).

Another difference from 'The Ordination of Presbyters . . .' is that the President is joined, at the laying on of hands, by a deacon. This is not a traditional practice, for to ordain has never been regarded as a diaconal function, but it was introduced in the 1989 service in response to strong representations from the Methodist Diaconal Order and retained in *The Methodist Worship Book*. Its supporters claim that it emphasizes the collegiality of diaconal ministry and the fact that deacons belong to a religious order. Those who do not think it appropriate for a deacon to be involved in the laying on of hands may take some comfort from the thought that it is the President who ordains, with the deacon exercising an assisting role (which, of course, is equally true of the presbyters who join the President in presbyteral ordinations).

Not all Methodist deacons are leaders of worship or preachers, and there is no clearly defined liturgical role for deacons in Methodism. *The Methodist Worship Book* does, however, assign to them traditional diaconal roles from the wider Church in 'The Easter Vigil' (p. 265, Note 4). Something similar happens in 'The Ordination of Deacons', where the ancient tradition of a deacon dismissing the people at the end of worship is maintained (35) when the Warden of the Methodist Diaconal Order says, 'Go in peace to love and serve the Lord.'

12

Admission, Commissioning and Welcome Services

For several years after 1975, *The Methodist Service Book* did not include any admission, commissioning or welcome services. Although such services were authorized by the Conference, and were always said to have the same status as those contained in the book, their omission from it was widely deplored. Later editions remedied the deficiency. Correspondents left the drafters of *The Methodist Worship Book* in no doubt that services of this sort must be included in the new book.

This section of *The Methodist Worship Book* contains a mixture of services, which, as will be shown below, have a wide range of roles to fulfil.

The Admission of Local Preachers

All Methodists are aware of the sterling work of Local Preachers. After their initial training, which takes place according to a Connexional scheme, but under the guidance and authority of the Circuit Local Preachers' Meeting, they must be approved by the Circuit Meeting before they can be admitted as accredited Local Preachers. The service of admission is therefore a very significant moment in any Local Preacher's life; and it is also a significant moment for all who share in this Circuit service. All this is indicated by the Introduction and the Notes (p. 329).

Although Local Preachers exercise a lay ministry and are not ordained, 'The Admission . . .' has a similar shape to the

Ordination Services. This is in part owing to the fact that, like ordination, admission as a Local Preacher happens only once.

After appropriate opening sentences (1) and a short prayer of adoration (3), there is a prayer of confession (4), adapted from the Australian *Uniting in Worship* (1988). It is the only text in this service to have been borrowed from another service book. The collect (5) leads to the Ministry of the Word, where a choice of readings is given for the Old Testament (6), the Epistle (8) and the Gospel (10).

The Admission falls into four sections. The first is the Presentation (13), which is rather like the Presentation in the two Ordination Services. In this instance, the Secretary of the Local Preachers' Meeting presents those who are to be admitted and states that they have been duly examined and have been approved by the Circuit Meeting. This is similar to what happens at an ordination, when the Secretary of the Conference or the Warden of the Methodist Diaconal Order presents candidates to the President and indicates that ordination is to take place on the authority of the Conference.

The second section is the Preface (14), in which the Superintendent addresses first the whole congregation and then specifically those who have been presented, setting the calling of Local Preachers within the context of the ministry of the whole Church.

Third, in the Questions (15), the Superintendent asks the candidates five questions, related to their calling, their faithfulness in matters of doctrine, discipline and study, and their personal discipleship, and the candidates reply accordingly. It is not too difficult to see the similarity between the Preface and the Questions in this service and the Examination in the Ordination Services.

Finally, the Admission proper takes place. The Superintendent (16) invites the Local Preachers who are present to stand as the candidates are admitted, and thus to reaffirm their own ministry. When they have done so, the rest of the congregation is invited to stand (17) and the Superintendent leads a prayer which begins with thanksgiving and proceeds to petition for those who are now being admitted as Local Preachers. There follows a sort of *porrectio instrumentorum* (see above, p. 125) when a Bible is presented to each new Local Preacher (18). Next (19) the people are asked to declare that they will support with their prayers those now admitted, faithfully share in the worship they lead, and receive through them the word of God.

The remainder of the service (20–23) consists entirely of rubrics, which deal with the reading of a letter from the President of the Conference, a copy of which is given to every new Local Preacher, the giving of the hand of fellowship, and the possibility of newly-admitted Local Preachers speaking about their calling. The final rubric gives directions for what should happen next if the Lord's Supper is to be celebrated (and it is best that it should be) and what should happen otherwise.

The Commissioning of Lay Workers

Local Preachers have played a significant part in Methodism from the earliest days, but Lay Workers, whose Commissioning Service we are now to consider, have only recently appeared on the scene. Largely as a result of a shortage of ministers and deacons, Circuits started to appoint lay people, with or without remuneration, to carry out various duties, usually, though by no means invariably, pastoral. What started in response to need proved to be very valuable in allowing fresh insights, gifts and energies to be offered to and through the Church. As more and more Lay Workers were appointed, the Conference introduced Standing Orders to provide some degree of consistency of practice and the necessary protections for both Lay Workers and Circuits. There remains, however, considerable diversity among the various Lay Worker appointments, as the Introduction (p. 336) makes plain. Most Lay Workers are appointed by Circuits, but some are appointed by Districts. Unlike Local Preachers, who are admitted for life, Lay Workers serve in appointments for limited periods. The Commissioning Service needs to be flexible and adaptable, given the many different circumstances in which its use may be required.

The first service for 'The Commissioning of Lay Workers' was authorized by the Conference of 1991. Little from that service has been carried forward into its successor, though the Commissioning (10) and some of the prayers (16) have been modelled on the earlier text.

The service is designed to be used during a celebration of the Lord's Supper, though material is provided for use when Holy Communion is not to be celebrated. In the collect (2), God's blessing is requested for the person to be commissioned and for all God's people, that his grace and glory may be made known to the world. The Ministry of the Word (3–9) follows the normal pattern.

All stand for the Commissioning. The presiding minister first presents the Lay Worker to the congregation (10) and indicates 'in a phrase' the duties he or she is to carry out. (The words 'in a phrase' were included to discourage the reading out of long and detailed job descriptions.) Then the presiding minister asks the Lay Worker three questions, which relate to vocation, discipline and faithfulness. Questions and answers of this nature are present in all the services in this section of *The Methodist Worship Book*. In a sense, they represent the divine calling to which human beings are invited to respond. Similarly, questions and answers play an important part in services of initiation and ordination.

Prayer is now offered (11) for the Lay Worker and her or his ministry, before (in a Circuit rather than a District appointment) a Circuit Steward asks the people (12) whether they will welcome, support, befriend and pray for the Lay Worker. It is right that a Circuit Steward should ask this question, for Lay Workers, like ministers, are appointed to Circuits, not to individual churches, even though they may work in only one or two churches. A local church welcome (13) may, however, be given by a representative and welcomes (14) may be given by other appropriate people. To all these, the newly-appointed Lay Worker may reply (15), in his or her own words and/or using the words:

I thank you for your welcome.
I will work with you and pray for you.

These words first appeared in the service of Welcome for a Minister which was published in 1975, independently of *The Methodist Service Book*. In that service, however, they were said several times, with the result that they came to lose their force. Used only once in a service, they retain their vitality.

Prayers of intercession (16) for the Church and the world are cast in the form of a number of biddings, each followed by a period of silence and a versicle and response. It was pointed out when the 1991 service was being prepared that any prayer containing biddings and using 'The Lord hears our prayer' as a versicle must include silences, for the biddings are not prayers but invitations to prayer.

After the Lord's Prayer (17) and the Peace (18), it is recommended (19) that the service should continue from the Preparation of the Gifts in one of the services of Holy Communion, that for 'the Day of Pentecost and Times of Renewal in the Life of the Church' being described as especially suitable.

A splendid prayer of thanksgiving and dedication (22) and a blessing (24) are printed for use if the Lord's Supper is not to be celebrated. It will be unfortunate if these texts are neglected (for the entirely laudable reason that this service will normally include Holy Communion). They could be used on many other occasions.

The Annual Commissioning of Pastoral Visitors and Class Leaders

Although *The Methodist Service Book* did not include a service for the commissioning of Class Leaders and Pastoral Visitors, such a service was authorized for use in 1975 and was regarded as being of the same status as the services in the service book.

Standing Order 631(2) makes it clear that those who are appointed to exercise pastoral responsibility for a group of people, but do not hold class meetings for them, are Pastoral Visitors. Relatively few churches now have such meetings, so it is appropriate that the Commissioning Service should refer to

Pastoral Visitors and Class Leaders, in that order, even though the latter is the older office.

This is the first of three closely related services, each of which is designed to be used after the sermon within the context of Holy Communion. All three services consist of a collect, a preface, and an act of commissioning.

The collect (1) asks God, who renews the strength of his servants, to fill them with his Spirit so that, in serving others, they may always be true to Christ. The Preface (2) begins with the statement that Pastoral Visitors (and Class Leaders) are to be commissioned. Then follow three pairs of responsive sentences, loosely based on 1 Corinthians 12 (especially verses 5 and 27), which amount to a declaration that all specific forms of Christian ministry are exercised within the one Body of Christ and are a sharing in Christ's ministry:

We are the Body of Christ:
each of us is a member of it.

There is one ministry of Christ:
in this ministry we all share.

There are different ways of serving God:
it is the same Lord whom we serve.

These sentences are used in all three of the closely linked commissioning services, providing a common text which testifies both to the essential unity and to the necessary diversity of Christian service.

The Preface continues with a brief description of the work of Pastoral Visitors and Class Leaders, which emphasizes that they exercise a ministry 'in the name of Christ and on behalf of the whole Church'. The concluding sentence, referring to the impossibility of the task without God's help, states that the Holy Spirit has been given to help and counsel us.

The Commissioning proper (3) now follows. Those who are to be commissioned are mentioned by name and they move to the front of the church, where the minister asks two questions about their sense of vocation and their commitment. A prayer for their empowerment by the Spirit is the central act of the Commissioning. It is followed (4) by the congregation pledging its encouragement and support and the offering of 'the hand of fellowship' (5). Tickets of membership (which are traditionally distributed by Class Leaders and Pastoral Visitors to those in their care) may then be given to them by the minister (6); whether or not this is done will probably be determined by the time of year when the service takes place.

The Annual Commissioning of Workers with Children and Young People

This service is so similar in structure and content to the previous one that it needs little comment. Unlike its predecessor from the 1970s, it is intended for annual use, rather than simply when new Workers are commissioned, though it may be used on those occasions as well.

Note 2 (p. 347) makes the important point that it is desirable for the children and young people of the church to be present when this service takes place. This is in order that they may be aware of the calling and commitment of those who work among them and of the whole Church's awareness of its responsibility for their nurture.

The opening collect (1), which refers to God's call to people from their earliest days, to human response, and to the making of disciples, is clearly appropriate on this occasion. It is based on a prayer written by the International Commission on English in the Liturgy. In the Preface (2), after the common responsive sentences discussed on p. 134 above, the ministry of Workers with Children and Young People is set within the context of the whole Church's responsibility for the young in fulfilment of the promises made at Baptism.

Two minor but not insignificant differences from the Pastoral Visitors' service may be noted. Those to be commissioned may be led from their places (3) by a child or a young person and a child or young person may lead the prayer (4) which is at the heart of the Commissioning. Both these options are intended to give children and young people an active role in the service and to demonstrate that they have a part to play within the church community.

The Commissioning of Worship Leaders

The third of the related acts of Commissioning very nearly did not appear in *The Methodist Worship Book*; indeed, no version of it was ever issued for trial use and it was not even included in the draft edition sent to members of the 1998 Conference. It was only when the draft edition had been distributed that it was suggested to the Faith and Order Committee by a member of the Conference that this omission ought to be remedied, because Standing Order 682(3) refers to such a service. The Faith and Order Committee took the point, and 'The Commissioning of Worship Leaders' was prepared in time for it to be printed in the second volume of the 1998 Conference *Agenda*.

In truth, it was not difficult to draw up this service fairly quickly, because it seemed obvious that it should share a family likeness with the services for Pastoral Visitors and Class Leaders and for Workers with Children and Young People. Unlike the latter, however, it is mainly intended for the commissioning of newly-accredited Worship Leaders, though it may also be adapted for use as an annual Commissioning Service.

The collect (1), fittingly, is about worship; it contains echoes of Hebrews 10.19f. and John 4.24. The remainder of the service follows the now-familiar pattern.

The Reception of Christians of other Communions into the Membership of the Methodist Church

It sometimes happens that a person who has been confirmed and/or received into membership in another branch of the

Christian Church wishes to be received into the membership of the Methodist Church. *The Methodist Service Book* gave detailed directions about what should be done in a variety of circumstances, directions which were no longer entirely appropriate following the decisions of the 1992 Conference, at which it was made clear that Methodist membership is always conferred during an act of worship, not when the Church Council votes in favour of a person being received into membership.

The Methodist Worship Book therefore needed to make liturgical provision for people who had previously been members of other denominations to become members of the Methodist Church. It seemed right to include this brief liturgy among the services of admission, commissioning and welcome, rather than in the 'Entry into the Church' section of the book, for this is not an initiation service.

The minister, after acknowledging that those to be received have been members of other Christian communions (1), asks whether they now wish to be Methodist members. After they have answered affirmatively, the minister says the words (2) always spoken when people are received into the membership of the Methodist Church; they can also be found, for example, on p. 72 of *The Methodist Worship Book*. On this occasion, however, a sentence of blessing follows before the minister and a representative of the local church extend the hand of fellowship to those who have been welcomed and received.

The questions and answers (4) are based on the texts in 'Entry into the Church'; they were amended in order to recognize the fact that those who have been received are often at a different stage in their Christian pilgrimage from those newly confirmed. It should be noted that these questions and answers *may* be included, but there will be circumstances when it is proper to omit them, for example when someone has been deeply involved in the life of the local church for many years, without being a member of it. As is customary, a promise (5) is made by the congregation.

It is interesting to note that there is another use to which this service, lightly amended, may be put. During the 1990s much consideration was given by several denominations and by some ecumenical bodies, such as Churches Together in England, to the possibility of 'extended membership', that is, the simultaneous membership of more than one denomination. The impetus for this consideration came from Local Ecumenical Partnerships, in which it is commonplace for people newly confirmed to enjoy membership of both or all the participating churches, whereas those people who have been involved from the outset remain members of only the one denomination. The latter was believed to be unsatisfactory, and all denominations were encouraged to seek ways, in keeping with their own understandings of membership, to extend membership to those of other churches within an ecumenical context.

Some other churches have responded positively to this appeal and the Methodist Conference resolved in 2000, and confirmed the decision in 2001, to amend the Deed of Union so as to make it clear that a Christian of another communion could become a member of the Methodist Church without being 'transferred' from the other communion. He or she could quite simply be a member of both churches. The Faith and Order Committee's report to the Conference of 2000 pointed out that the service which we are considering could be used for the reception and welcome of such a person, provided that two small modifications were made to the opening words (1). Instead of

> N *and* N *(N)*, you have been *members* of *other communions* within the Church of Christ. Do you now wish to be *members* of the Methodist Church?

the minister should say:

> N *and* N *(N)*, you are *members* of *other communions* within the Church of Christ. Do you wish also to be *members* of the Methodist Church?

Unfortunately, these new provisions came too late to be included in *The Methodist Worship Book*.

The Welcome of Ministers, Deacons and Probationers

Each September, many ministers, deacons and probationers take up new appointments. As the Introduction (p. 355) explains, services to mark these new beginnings are regarded as services of welcome. The term 'induction', which has sometimes been borrowed from other denominations and used by Methodists in recent years, is not an accurate description of Methodist practice, since all appointments are made by the Conference.

The Liturgical Sub-Committee's decision that one service should be prepared which would be suitable whether ministers, deacons, probationers, or some combination of these were to be welcomed, did not prove easy to put into effect and there are some places (for example on p. 358) where the rubrics need to be read very carefully in order to get things right.

The prayer of adoration and invocation (3), like almost every text in this service, was newly composed for *The Methodist Worship Book*. It is a remarkable prayer, which could fittingly be used at the start of any act of worship or, indeed, as a prayer in the vestry. It is followed by a rather short and terse act of confession (4), which nevertheless manages to express penitence for failures in listening for God's word, in the use of God's gifts, and in the Church's common life, service and evangelism.

After the Ministry of the Word, which follows the familiar pattern and for which suitable Bible readings are suggested, comes a section called 'The Presentation, Promises and Welcome'. The first two elements of this take one of two forms, depending upon whether it is presbyters and/or probationers for presbyteral ministry who are being welcomed, or deacons and/or probationers for diaconal ministry.

In the case of the former, the presiding minister presents the newly-appointed presbyter or probationer to the people, with appropriate words (13). An Appendix (pp. 365f.) supplies a text to be used before these words if a minister already stationed in the Circuit has now been appointed as its Superintendent.

The three promises (14) are so structured that they are like a three-way conversation involving the presiding minister, the newly-appointed person and the whole congregation. First, the presiding minister asks the newly-appointed person a question regarding his or her role. Then the new minister responds affirmatively, asks for God's help, and invites those present to join him or her in the fulfilment of those aspects of ministry. Each time, the people respond with an affirmation or a prayer. It should be noted that in some early editions of the book, the red asterisk which ought to be alongside the line 'presides at the Lord's Supper' is missing. This is the line to which reference is made in a note at the foot of p. 358.

If a newly-appointed presbyter is the new Superintendent, there is a further question (15) related to the specific duties of that office.

The Presentation and Promises for deacons and probationers for diaconal ministry (16, 17) are very similar to those which we have just considered. Indeed, the words spoken in response to the questions and the congregation's words (17) are identical. But because of the differences between presbyteral and diaconal ministry, the first two questions asked by the presiding minister are different.

Welcomes now follow, beginning with a welcome from the whole congregation (18), prompted by a Circuit Steward. Circuit Stewards have particular responsibilities in relation to ministers and deacons in their Circuits, and it is entirely fitting that a Circuit Steward should invite the people to welcome those newly appointed and to promise friendship, support and prayers.

Further welcomes (19) may be given by those mentioned in the rubrics, and the 1975 response, discussed on pp. 132f. above, may be said in reply. The prayers of intercession (21) are identical to those in 'The Commissioning of Lay Workers'; they are equally appropriate in both services, and indeed are among the prayers which could be used on other occasions too.

After the Lord's Prayer (22) and the Peace (23), it is desirable for the service to continue from the Preparation of the Gifts in one of the services of Holy Communion, and a rubric (24) gives advice about this. If the Lord's Supper is not to be celebrated, the printed prayer of thanksgiving (26) or some other prayer should be said. Like its equivalent in 'The Commissioning of Lay Workers', this prayer is also suitable for use at other times.

The services in this section of the book are designed for a range of different occasions, but they are united by two common features. In all of them, solemn promises are made by individuals and in all of them, the whole congregation promises to support and pray for those individuals.

13

Marriage and the Blessing of a Marriage

The Introduction (p. 367) describes both the solemnity and the joy that characterize marriage as Christians understand it and explains the relationship between the two services included in this section of *The Methodist Worship Book*.

The Marriage Service

No Notes in the book were more difficult to write than those on pp. 367f. Clearly it was essential that adequate information should be given about the requirements of the law, but because these requirements vary in different places where *The Methodist Worship Book* is used, it was necessary also to draw attention to the need for ministers to ensure compliance with the relevant requirements. To compare Note 2 (p. 368) with its equivalent in *The Methodist Service Book* is to be reminded of how much has changed in a quarter of a century; it would have been completely unacceptable in 1999 to say simply, 'Other legal provisions may apply outside England'!

The Marriage Service prepared for the new book is a striking mixture of the traditional and the innovative. It begins (1) with a statement of what is to happen during the service, though this may be preceded by informal words of welcome. The prayer of confession (3) is one of very few texts borrowed from the 1975 service and it has been slightly amended. Its strength lies in the fact that, though it properly expresses penitence for human ingratitude and the misuse of God's gifts, that penitence is set within the context of God's generous love. On such a joyful occasion, it is right that confession and thanksgiving should intermingle as they do in this prayer.

What in 1975 was known as the Declaration of Purpose, and addressed to the congregation, has been replaced by an untitled address (4) to the persons to be married. This is a clear and unambiguous statement of the Christian understanding of marriage. Its final paragraph has a strongly Trinitarian flavour, always appropriate, but especially in this context, for the Trinity is a unity of love.

The legal declarations (5) take advantage of the recent changes in marriage law in England and Wales, which allow for any one of three texts to be used at this point. The one included in the body of the service consists of a question addressed to each party, to which he or she simply replies, 'I am.' The other permitted forms of words are printed in an Appendix (p. 384); the first of them is the traditional 'I do solemnly declare . . .' which for generations has been a cause of stumbling to many who have had to say it. The other text is a simplified form of those words.

A declaration of intention to marry (6) is now made by both parties, again by means of questions and answers. It is at this early point in the service that a version of the familiar words 'Will you love her/him, comfort and honour her/him . . . ?' is included, rather than immediately before the 'contracting words' (13). Having declared that they are free lawfully to marry, it seems fitting that the two parties should immediately declare their intention to do so, and promise to love and be faithful to each other throughout their lives.

Ideally the Ministry of the Word (7–9) will follow, though provision is made, as it was in the previous service book, for some or all of it to be deferred until after the proclamation that the couple are married (15). It is liturgically preferable for vows to be made after the reading and exposition of Scripture, but for pastoral reasons it is sometimes desirable to defer the Ministry of the Word.

Six Scripture passages (7) are set out in the body of the service and a further eighteen possible readings are listed on p. 398. There is clearly an abundance of readings from which to choose; it would be unusual to have more than two or three, the last of which should be a Gospel reading if Holy Communion is to follow.

As the section of the service entitled 'The Marriage' begins, all stand (10) and the minister asks the families and friends of the couple to promise to do all in their power 'to support and encourage them in their marriage'. This is a new feature of the service, roughly parallel to the sort of promise made by congregations at Baptism (see, for example, p. 70 of *The Methodist Worship Book*) or in services of commissioning (as on p. 339). The inclusion of the people's promise is to be welcomed. Marriage is more than a relationship between two people; it exists within the context of a wider society and other people can help to enrich it or in fact to destroy it.

After the people's promise, there is provision for one or both of the parties to be presented for marriage (11). This innovation was warmly welcomed when it was included in the draft Marriage Service which was issued for trial use. It is an attempt to address the problem created by two quite different approaches to the traditional 'giving away' of the bride. On the one hand, there has long been a feeling that the giving away ('Who gives this woman to be married to this man?') is demeaning to women, an unpleasant survival from the days in which women were regarded almost as items of property, transferable from one man (the bride's father) to another (the husband). On the other hand, experience shows that many women regard this ceremony as important, despite its origins, partly because it is traditional and partly because they want their father or some other close relation or friend to have this role to fulfil. How in the late twentieth century could these two views be reconciled?

The proposed solution is ingenious. For a start, the relevant part of the service (11) is entirely optional. Couples who want nothing to do with anything that in any way resembles a 'giving away' need not include it. Second, the word 'give' is avoided and 'present' is used instead: 'Who presents *C* to be married to *A*?'

'Presenting' is quite different from 'giving'. Third, it is possible for both parties to be treated in exactly the same way; the man, as well as the woman, may be presented for marriage by a relative or friend. Thus there are three possibilities: one party may be presented, two parties may be presented or neither may be presented. Both those who object to any vestige of the traditional 'giving away' and those who want to preserve something of that traditional ceremony are catered for.

After a prayer (12), which is borrowed from *The Methodist Service Book*, the Vows (13) are made. They begin with the simplest version of the words required at this point by law (in England and Wales): 'I, AB/CD, take you, CD/AB, to be my wedded wife/husband.' The Appendix (p. 384) indicates the other legally permitted forms of these 'contracting' words.

The remaining words of the Vows are a gently modernized version of the traditional words, 'for better, for worse . . .' There has been some change in the order of the phrases and some rather archaic constructions (such as the words 'till death us do part', which were not always said correctly) have been replaced by their more modern equivalents (such as 'until we are parted by death'), but enough remains of the traditional words for the Vows to have a familiar feel.

The Giving of the Ring(s) (14) provides for a number of options. In recent years, a mutual exchange of rings has become more common, though it still happens from time to time that only the bride will be given a ring. The left-hand column indicates what should happen if there are two rings; the right-hand column deals with the case of one ring. Whether there is one ring or two, the minister receives the ring(s) on the book which she or he is holding and says a prayer of blessing. In *The Methodist Service Book*, at the equivalent point, God was asked to bless 'the giving' of the ring(s), but here there is an unequivocal 'bless this (these) ring(s)'. Some may feel that it is inappropriate to ask for the blessing of inanimate objects, but the remainder of the prayer makes it clear that God is being asked to bless each ring in order that it may be a symbol of the couple's love and trust. The wearing of a wedding ring is a perpetual reminder to the one who wears it, and to others, that the wearer is committed in marriage to another person. Stories have been told about people who have come close to breaking their marriage vows, but have been stopped short by the sight of their wedding rings. It does not therefore seem improper to ask God's blessing on what can be such enduringly powerful symbols.

If there are two rings, they may be given in one of two ways. The man may place a ring on the woman's ring finger and say appropriate words to her, after which the woman places a ring on the man's ring finger and says identical words to him; or the rings may be given and the man and the woman may say a sentence (borrowed from *The Methodist Service Book*) together. Similar options are provided for occasions when there is only one ring, except that, on receipt of the ring that has been presented to the woman with the words 'I give you this ring . . .', she replies, 'I receive this ring . . .' The choice to be made at this point will need to be discussed in advance between the couple and the minister: the determining consideration should be to use the form with which the man and the woman are more comfortable.

The proclamation of the marriage (15) begins with the minister joining the right hands of the man and the woman, as is traditional. The rubric allows for a stole to be wrapped around their joined hands – a possibility that would not have been envisaged in 1975! Then the minister addresses the man and the woman:

> *A* and *C*, God so join you together that none shall ever part you.

This sentence echoes Matthew 19.6. In previous liturgies, there has been a straight quotation of the biblical words, used as a sort of admonition, as in the sonorous words of *The Book of Common Prayer* (1662):

> Those whom God hath joined together let no man put asunder.

With the substitution of 'has' for 'hath', these words were in-cluded in *The Methodist Service Book*. The earliest unpublished drafts of the new service used a version of this sentence (in non-exclusive language) in the same sort of way, but it was decided that a better way to echo the biblical text would be as words addressed to the couple rather than as an admonition to the people. Interestingly, however, the sentence comes in the same place, before the formal pronouncement of the marriage, as it does in *The Book of Common Prayer*, rather than after it (as in *The Methodist Service Book* and *The Alternative Service Book* [1980]).

The minister now declares that, having exchanged vows, joined hands, and given and received a ring or rings, the man and the woman are married. Though a hymn (16) may be sung at this point, it is better to defer it until after the blessing of the couple (17) so that the latter may immediately follow the proclamation of the marriage.

Now is the time (18) for the Ministry of the Word, or part of it, if it has not already taken place. The prayers of intercession (19) are mainly petitions for the husband and wife and for their marriage, but they conclude with a prayer for all present and (20) the Lord's Prayer. If Holy Communion is not to be celebrated, there is a prayer of thanksgiving (22) and a blessing (24). The prayer is a major revision of the final thanksgiving in the Marriage Service of *The Methodist Service Book*, though it has a clearer Trinitarian structure and is much more concise than the older text. The rubric which introduces the blessing makes it clear that the words are addressed to all present, unlike the earlier blessing (17) which was addressed only to the newly-married couple. The left-hand version is the Aaronic Blessing (see above, p. 67); the right-hand version is Psalm 67.1.

Most Marriage Services will end in this way, for it is relatively rare for Holy Communion to be celebrated at Methodist wed-dings. Even when the people being married are regular com-municants, many of their family and friends may not be, and a eucharistic conclusion to the service may be considered divisive. One solution to this problem (also sometimes adopted on the dubious ground that it saves time) is for only the presiding minister and the couple to receive communion, but this is unsatisfactory, because at every celebration of this sacrament all communicants who are present ought to be able to receive. The rubrics in *The Methodist Worship Book* assume that the latter will be the case.

On the relatively infrequent occasions when Holy Communion is to be celebrated, the Peace (25) is shared and at the Preparation of the Gifts (26) the usual rubric is modified by the suggestion that the husband and wife, or other members of the congregation, may bring bread and wine to the table. The Great Prayer of Thanksgiving (27) has a strongly Trinitarian preface, in which the themes of human love, family life, and companionship are given prominent expression. There is a modification of the usual rubric about the Sharing of the Bread and Wine (30) to provide for the husband and wife and their families to be the next to receive, after the presiding minister. This is the only place in the book where there is an unambiguous direction that the presiding minister should receive first (see above, p. 79). After the familiar post-communion prayer (34), used also in 'Holy Communion for Ordinary Seasons (First Service)', the service concludes with the same blessing (36) that would have been said had there been no communion.

The Blessing of a Marriage Previously Solemnized

The Notes (p. 385) make clear what this service is not! It is not suitable for the solemnization of marriage, or for the reaffirmation or renewal of marriage vows. As the Introduction (p. 367) has already stated, 'it is intended for those whose marriage was solemnized in a civil ceremony and who later desire the blessing of that marriage in an act of Christian worship'.

In the preparation of this service, two considerations in particular needed to be kept in mind. First, and obviously, nothing must be included that would already have taken place in the civil marriage ceremony. Second, however, the purpose of the service is to seek, in the context of Christian worship, God's blessing on a marriage that has already taken place. The service should therefore resemble 'The Marriage Service' as much as possible, because it is in the latter that, alongside the words required by law, the Christian understanding of marriage is set forth.

'The Blessing . . .' takes due account of these two considerations. Because the couple are already married, some texts from 'The Marriage Service' required slight alteration before they could be included in 'The Blessing . . .' An example is the final paragraph of the address (3) which may be compared with its equivalent (4) in the previous service. But wherever possible, the same words are used, for example in the prayer of thanksgiving (17) and the eucharistic liturgy (20–31). The content of the two services is so similar, and the reasons for the differences between the two so obvious, that no further discussion of 'The Blessing . . .' is needed here.

14

Pastoral Services

Nothing resembling the two services in this section of *The Methodist Worship Book* appeared in its 1975 predecessor, though earlier versions of each of them were prepared by the Faith and Order Committee (in response to a Connexional debate on 'Christian Initiation' in the 1980s) and authorized by the Conference of 1989. A number of issues related to Baptism had not only prompted the preparation of the report, 'Christian Initiation', but had also led to the conclusion that 'new and additional rites' were needed.

The issues relevant to these 'new rites' were as follows. Despite the fact that the Methodist Church insisted, and still insists, that infant Baptism (now generally known as the Baptism of young children) is true Baptism, it was clear that some Methodist parents were reluctant to have their children baptized. Their reading of the New Testament suggested to them that Baptism should be administered only when a person was able to speak for himself or herself and to make a personal response of faith in Christ. In calling for a service of thanksgiving after the birth or adoption of a child, the Conference was not abandoning its position on infant Baptism, but was seeking to accommodate those who wished to give thanks for their child without having him or her baptized.

At the same time, there was continuing unease in the Church about what its supporters call 'open Baptism' and its critics 'indiscriminate Baptism'. Congregations had often been puzzled or dismayed by the fact that families, previously unknown to them, had come to church for the Baptism of a child and had never subsequently returned, unless for the Baptism of a further child. Some Methodists take the view that Baptism should not be withheld from any child at least one of whose parents requests it and is willing to answer the questions put to her or him. Others believe that only when at least one parent is a practising Christian, involved in the life of the local church, should an infant be baptized.

It was felt that the provision of a service which was not Baptism, but which marked the birth or adoption of a child, would both enable the Church to safeguard the significance of the sacrament of Baptism and also allow parents to celebrate the arrival of their child without making the commitments entailed in Baptism.

The 'Act of Thanksgiving after the Birth or Adoption of a Child', therefore, is designed to meet two quite different pastoral needs. To put it rather crudely, it is intended to meet the needs of those parents whom the Church would not hesitate to regard as suitable to present their children for Baptism, but who do not themselves wish to have their children baptized because they are uneasy about infant Baptism. It is also designed for those who are not ready or willing to make the commitments associated with Baptism.

A third issue, related to the other two, came to prominence in the closing decades of the twentieth century. What happens if a person, baptized in childhood, and maybe having had little or no contact with the Church, comes at a later stage to a living faith in Christ and believes that this newly-found faith should be professed in Baptism? The position of the Methodist Church is clear and uncompromising: 'It is contrary to the principles and usage of the Methodist Church to confer what purports to be Baptism on any person known to have been already baptized at any time' (Standing Order 010A[5]). The Standing Order is right to insist that 'rebaptism' should not take place. Baptism, like birth, is unrepeatable. But what other options are open to a person who has long since been baptized and who now wishes to make a public profession of faith? Various suggestions have been made. Confirmation would clearly be appropriate in some cases (though obviously not if the person has already been confirmed).

Sharing in the Covenant Service may be seen as a means of renewing the baptismal Covenant (though the Covenant Service is likely to be regarded as too much an act of public worship and insufficiently closely related to the individual's own faith journey). 'A Celebration of Christian Renewal' was specifically designed to be used in these circumstances.

It is not difficult to see, therefore, why this section of the book is entitled 'Pastoral Services'. Both services came into existence in response to perceived pastoral needs. How often they will be used, whether the need for their use will increase or diminish, whether or not any new version of one or both of them will ever be produced – these are questions that remain to be answered.

An Act of Thanksgiving after the Birth or Adoption of a Child

The Introduction (p. 399) mentions those occasions for which this service may be suitable which have been discussed above, and also some other occasions (such as when an adopted child has already been baptized). The Note on the same page indicates where 'An Act of Thanksgiving . . .' is best situated within a full act of worship.

The collect (2) makes reference to the earthly home of Jesus in Nazareth and prays that the child and her/his family may be united with God and with one another. After two appropriate Scripture passages (3), the minister asks the name of the child (4) before leading a prayer of thanksgiving (5) for God's mighty acts in creation and redemption and for the gift of the child. The final paragraph is a prayer for the child that he or she may come to know God, be initiated into the Christian community, be nurtured with the bread of life and share in the joys of God's kingdom. The fact that all this can be encompassed in only six lines is remarkable.

The parents are now asked (6) whether they thankfully receive the child as a gift from God and promise to love and care for him or her. A further question may be asked (7), which concerns the sharing of faith with the child and praying with him or her. This question may well be suitable for parents who are practising Christians, but it is less appropriate for those who are unwilling or unable to make the commitments which Baptism would entail. That is why the question is optional.

As in so many services, the people are now invited to make a promise (8), in this case to surround and support the family with love and prayer. (This is one of a very few places in *The Methodist Worship Book* where the grammar may be questioned. Since 'family' is a singular noun, the pronoun in the next line should, strictly speaking, be 'it' rather than 'them'. But the English language is slowly changing; it is now regarded as acceptable for a spokesperson to say, 'The Government are determined to . . .' or 'The Committee have agreed . . .' Perhaps in the present context, the word 'them', while regrettable to a grammatical purist, is warmer than the impersonal 'it' and therefore acceptable.)

The minister may now take the child (9) in his or her arms. Whether or not this is done, there is a prayer that God will bless the child. After the optional giving of a Bible (10), there are short intercessions (11) for the family and for all present, before 'An Act of Thanksgiving . . .' concludes with the Lord's Prayer (12) and a blessing (13). The latter is an abridgement of a blessing which was written for *The Alternative Service Book* (1980), though a reference to this source has unfortunately been omitted from the Acknowledgements (p. 603).

Unlike some other service books, which situate similar liturgies among their initiation services, *The Methodist Worship Book* has deliberately put a considerable amount of paper between 'Entry into the Church' and 'An Act of Thanksgiving . . .' It was believed to be important to do everything possible to avoid any confusion between this service and 'The Baptism of Young Children' and to make clear that the focus of 'An Act of Thanksgiving . . .' is pastoral rather than initiatory.

A Celebration of Christian Renewal

Although the circumstances described at the beginning of this
chapter led to the production of an earlier version of 'A Celebration of Christian Renewal' in 1989, the Introduction (p. 404)
indicates that there are other significant occasions that may
appropriately be marked by the use of this short act. The second
paragraph of the Introduction is worth careful perusal. It
explains that, although the service marks a significant individual
experience, this should not be seen in isolation from the life of
the whole Christian community. This link between personal
experience and the Church's corporate life is given expression in
the service itself. The Note (p. 404) sets the service within the
context of Holy Communion.

The opening sentences (1) start with a paraphrase of a verse
from the *Magnificat* (Luke 1.49) and continue with an explanation of what is to follow. Then the person whose renewal is being
celebrated (referred to as N in the service and, hereafter, in these
comments) is asked a number of questions (2). These relate to
faith and experience of God, Father, Son and Holy Spirit, to a
desire to love God and neighbour, and to faithfulness in prayer,
Scripture reading, and in the Church's worship and fellowship.
To each question N answers, 'Yes, I do.' The inclusion of the
word 'yes', alongside the more usual 'I do', may seem strange in
a liturgical context, but it was included in order to make the
answers sound less 'churchy' and formal than might otherwise
have been the case.

There is provision for N to give a testimony (3) and declare
commitment to Christ. It seems likely that most people for whom
this service is designed will want to take this opportunity, though
that will not invariably be the case. Whether or not there is testimony, the minister (4) assures N of the Church's rejoicing with
him or her and its prayer for God's continuing blessing. A blessing (5) may be accompanied by the laying on of hands, that
ancient sign with multiple significance which has been discussed
in Chapter Seven. A prayer (6) thanking God for what has been

done in N's life and praying for N's future spiritual development (or an extempore prayer) may be followed by an invitation (7) to others to commit their lives to Christ. 'Altar calls' are much rarer in present-day Methodism than was once the case, and this is the only place in *The Methodist Worship Book* where such a thing is specifically suggested (though it is nowhere precluded). The circumstances of the occasion will determine whether or not it is appropriate to make this invitation.

Finally, the whole congregation renews its Christian commitment in a prayer (8) inspired by Romans 12.1. In these closing words, the focus shifts from individual experience and the 'internal' life of the Church to mission and service and God's eternal kingdom.

15

Healing and Reconciliation Services

By now, readers may well be weary of being told that nothing equivalent to this or that section of *The Methodist Worship Book* was provided in *The Methodist Service Book*, but that is once again the case with the three services that we are about to consider.

An Order of Service for Healing and Wholeness

Since the publication of *The Methodist Service Book* there has been greater interest among Methodists in the ministry of healing, and, in the absence of any authorized or recommended liturgies for 'healing services', many local liturgies were developed, or services held with very little discernible structure and sometimes with questionable content. The Introduction (p. 407) explains what is meant in *The Methodist Worship Book* by a Service for Healing and Wholeness. It was carefully written in order to dispel any fears or false expectations about the nature of the service and to emphasize that the focus of the service is on God, 'who desires wholeness of body, mind and spirit for all people'.

Either the laying on of hands or anointing with oil, or both, may feature in this service. As we have seen in previous chapters, the laying on of hands is a practice which can occur in a number of different circumstances, with its precise significance always being determined by the context. In connection with healing and wholeness, there is scriptural warrant for it, for example in Mark 6.5 and 16.18. Anointing with oil is associated with healing in James 5.14, but there is no other evidence of the use of oil in connection with healing until the early third century – a sufficiently early date, however, to justify the assertion in the Introduction that anointing is a practice of the early Church. The Notes (pp. 407f.) give guidance as to how the laying on of hands and the anointing should be done and sensibly direct that appropriate information should be given to the congregation before the service starts.

The service is designed to be used in the context of a celebration of Holy Communion, its most fitting setting (St Ignatius of Antioch, martyred in the early second century, called the Eucharist 'the medicine of immortality'), but provision is made for occasions when the Lord's Supper will not be celebrated.

Opening sentences (1) are followed by a collect which immediately sets the tone for the service. It puts into words the concepts of the God in whom all things are made whole, who gave his Son to heal a broken world, and of human beings being blessed in body, mind and spirit. The prayer of confession (4) also addresses these themes; it is followed by the collect of the day (5) or a simple collect which asks God to give peace to the worshippers.

If anointing is to take place, a prayer (6) is said over the oil. Although God is asked to bless the oil 'for the healing of the sick', the prayer goes on to make direct intercession for those who will be anointed.

Anyone who is dubious about the place of services of healing and wholeness in the life of the Church may be encouraged to recognize the value of such services by noting how many possible Scripture readings are listed (8, 10, 12) in the Ministry of the Word. It will often be most satisfactory to choose an Old Testament reading, an Epistle and a Gospel from among these suggested passages, although the rubrics are worded in such a way as to imply that the Lectionary readings for the day should be regarded as the 'default' passages.

The prayers of intercession (15) were skilfully crafted so as to relate petitions for those in need to the birth, life, ministry, death and resurrection of Jesus; for example:

Christ, tested in the desert,
give courage to those who are tempted . . .

Christ, who hung in agony on the cross,
bring strength to those who suffer.

The printed prayers may be preceded by other prayers, and this
may be desirable if there are specific concerns which ought to be
mentioned. In churches where this service will be rarely, if ever,
used, it would be a pity for these lovely prayers to be neglected;
they could perfectly well be included in other services.

After the prayers, the laying on of hands and/or the anointing
with oil takes place (16) if the Lord's Supper is not to be celebrated, and may occur at this point even if there is to be communion, though in these circumstances it may be thought better
to defer such acts (to 29). It is normal, though not essential, for
those who are to lay hands on others and/or to anoint to receive
the laying on of hands and/or anointing themselves first. One
of three printed sentences may be said as the action takes place.
The third, which is especially beautiful, is 'borrowed' from the
Scottish *Book of Common Order* (1994), but is thought to
predate that book. The other sentences were written by the
Liturgical Sub-Committee.

The Peace follows (17) and, if there is to be a celebration of
the Lord's Supper, the Great Prayer of Thanksgiving (21). In
the clearly Trinitarian preface, where God is addressed as
'Gracious', 'Redeeming' and 'Holy', there is more opportunity
than is usual in this part of the prayer for congregational
responses. The remainder of the prayer is relatively brief, though
all the usual ingredients of a eucharistic thanksgiving are present.

If the laying on of hands and/or anointing has not taken place
earlier, it follows the Sharing of the Bread and Wine (26). The
normal practice in this case is for those who wish to avail themselves of this ministry to wait at the rail after receiving communion, while those who do not so wish return to their seats. It
would, however, be possible for all to return to their seats after
communicating, and for an invitation then to be issued for

people to come to the rail again for the laying on of hands and/or anointing. Local circumstances will suggest which method is more appropriate.

The post-communion prayer (32) is reminiscent of the equivalent prayer in 'Holy Communion during Ordinary Seasons (Third Service)'. Two forms of the blessing are provided – the Aaronic Blessing (see above, p. 67) and the opening verse of Psalm 67.

If there is no communion, a prayer of thanksgiving (36) is said. This bears a very close resemblance to the responsive sections of the Preface in the Great Prayer of Thanksgiving (21). After the Lord's Prayer, a final collect (38) is said by all. This prayer is based on a passage from the opening sentences of the *Confessions* of St Augustine of Hippo (354–430). It appeared as the collect for the Eighteenth Sunday after Pentecost in *The Methodist Service Book*, but, rather surprisingly, it is not used as a Sunday collect in *The Methodist Worship Book*. The blessing (40) and dismissal (41) are identical to those with which the service concludes when the Lord's Supper is celebrated.

A Service of Repentance and Reconciliation

Although confession (in the sense of individuals regularly confessing their sins to another person) has not been a common feature of Methodism, many ministers and others have met people who have wished to make a confession and to unburden themselves of a sense of guilt. As the Introduction (p. 422) states: 'an act of confession and declaration of forgiveness may be an important step towards reconciliation, spiritual growth and wholeness'.

Until 1999, Methodists had no form of worship which could be used in these circumstances, but *The Methodist Worship Book* supplies a short service for the purpose. Anyone who proposes to use it should carefully read the Introduction and Notes.

Although presbyters are appropriate people to lead this service, they have no exclusive claim to do so. It had been intended that this point should be made by the omission of any reference to 'the minister' in the rubrics – an intention which was carried out except in rubric 8, where the inclusion of the term seems to have been overlooked!

After a greeting (1) and the Lord's Prayer (2) 1 John 1.8–9 is read (3); it may be followed by another reading selected from a long list. Then follows the Act of Repentance and Reconciliation proper.

The minister or other person who is to hear the confession sets what is to follow in the context of God's help (4), and the penitent person makes a general confession (5) and then a specific confession. Guidance or counsel (6) may then be offered; Note 2 (p. 422) has some advice to offer about this. The penitent now asks for God's forgiveness in a prayer which is based on the confession from 'Holy Communion during Ordinary Seasons (First Service)' (pp. 185f.). This done, the person who has heard the confession declares the penitent's sin forgiven (8). The closing words of dismissal (9) very properly ask the penitent to pray for the person who has heard the confession, who is also a sinner in need of God's forgiveness.

This service, which is deeply indebted to the tradition of the wider Church, may not often be required among Methodists, but on an occasion when there is a pastoral need for someone to make confession to God in the presence of another person, it can be a true means of grace.

Prayer with the Dying

Some readers may think it strange that 'Prayer with the Dying' has been included among the 'Healing and Reconciliation Services', but as the Introduction suggests (p. 426), such prayer 'may be part of the process of reconciliation with God'. The provision of this act of worship will be a great boon to ministers and others who are called upon to pray with a person close to death. The Note (p. 426) helpfully points out that the manner in which the service is used will vary according to circumstances.

Two opening sentences (1) are provided, of which at least one is said. The first, which is indebted to 1 Samuel 25.6 and Luke 10.5, has a very long association with this type of service; it was used, for example in 'The Order for the Visitation of the Sick' in *The Book of Common Prayer* (1662). The second sentence is the Grace. One or two further short passages of Scripture (Philippians 4.5b–7; Matthew 11.28) may follow (2). A short prayer (3) for the blessing and comfort of the dying person is said. This prayer comes from the Australian *Uniting in Worship* (1988).

One of three Psalms follows (4). The first two are fairly obvious choices: Psalm 23 is the best known of all Psalms, and its very familiarity suggests that it will often be the appropriate choice, especially if the sick person is not able to register any response. Psalm 121, which eloquently testifies to God's care and protection, is also clearly suitable for such an occasion. The two verses from Psalm 131, however, are a less obvious choice, and indeed they were not included in the service until its final revision by the Faith and Order Committee. But for those who, in this service, are 'calming and quieting their souls', these verses could not be more apt.

Confession (5) is a fitting ingredient of this service, but it may sometimes be necessary to confine it to a very brief act; *Kyries* are provided for this purpose. The alternative is a revised version of a corporate confession from *The Alternative Service Book* (1980), followed by a declaration of forgiveness.

The canticle *Nunc Dimittis* (The Song of Simeon) (6), which was discussed in Chapter Five, takes on a new significance (or perhaps something closer to its biblical significance) by being included here. In Luke's account, the elderly Simeon, to whom it has been revealed that he will not die before seeing the Messiah, rejoices that God is allowing him to 'depart in peace' after encountering the child Jesus in the temple.

Two short prayers (7) are supplied; either or both of them may be said, according to circumstances, though provision is also made for extempore prayer. The first printed prayer is for the sick, the suffering and the dying; the second is for the dying person's friends and family. The Lord's Prayer (8) follows.

There is a choice of commendations (9). The first, 'Go forth upon your journey', is familiar to countless Methodists because of its inclusion in Newman's *The Dream of Gerontius*, as set to music by Sir Edward Elgar. This text, technically known as *Proficiscere*, is derived from the Roman Catholic rite of Extreme Unction and has long been associated with prayer with those who are dying.

For both the other commendations *The Methodist Worship Book* is once more indebted to *Uniting in Worship* (1988). The first of these (9B) is clearly influenced by *Proficiscere*, though it is sufficiently different from that ancient text to stand alone. The second (9C) is a short commendatory prayer for the dying person.

The service ends with a familiar blessing (10), based on Philippians 4.7.

16

Funeral and Related Services

To compare the 70 pages of *The Methodist Worship Book* which are devoted to 'Funeral and Related Services' with the equivalent section of *The Methodist Service Book*, which allocates only 21 (much smaller) pages to such services, is to recognize how much more comprehensive the present book is than its predecessor. As was noted on p. 4 above, the substantial provision of material in this section was a direct result of requests which had been received over many years.

In the Table of Contents (p. iv), the layout is intended to make clear that the 'Funeral and Related Services' fall into three subsections. First, there are three short services which may be used before a funeral; second, there are four funeral services; third, there is a service for the burial of ashes. A list of additional Scripture readings is also provided.

Prayers in the Home or Hospital after a Death

Ministers or pastoral visitors, calling at a home or arriving at a hospital in which someone has died, will often be asked, or will offer, to pray with the family and friends who are present. Although many ministers, in particular, will want to pray extempore or will have developed their own sets of prayers for such occasions, *The Methodist Worship Book* provides a short service which may be used instead. Apart from the person leading the service, no one will normally need a copy of it, since the only text to be spoken by everyone present is the Lord's Prayer.

The opening sentence (1) sets the present time of sorrow in the context of Christ's beatitude to those who mourn (Matthew 5.4). It is followed by silent prayer. Then (2) verses from John 14, or some other Scripture passage, may be read. The Lord's Prayer follows (3).

Three further prayers are provided (4), during the saying of one or more of which, according to the rubric, the sign of the cross may be made on the forehead of the person who has died. The signing will most appropriately accompany the first prayer, though it would not be inappropriate with the second. It does not, however, fit comfortably with the third, which is a prayer for the bereaved.

The first and third prayers are original compositions but the second is a translation of the *Kontakion* for the Dead, for which *The Methodist Worship Book* is indebted to the Orthodox tradition. The first paragraph, repeated at the end, is a *kontakion* in its own right, and is used in Orthodox daily prayer. There are many different translations of the *Kontakion* for the Dead; the one printed here is identical with that in *The Book of Alternative Services* (1985) of the Anglican Church of Canada, though this is not mentioned in the Acknowledgements.

The inclusion of this *kontakion* illustrates once again the rich diversity of sources which underlie *The Methodist Worship Book*.

This short act of worship concludes with the blessing (5), 'The peace of God, which passes all understanding . . .' (based on Philippians 4.7), which appears, sometimes as an option, in almost every service in this section. Not only is it obviously appropriate here, but its use provides a link with the funeral service which is yet to happen.

An Office of Commendation

The Note (p. 437) gives an indication of the uses to which 'An Office of Commendation' may be put. It may be said privately, or by a group of people who have heard of a death. Anecdotal evidence suggests that this office has already started to meet a need.

It begins with sentences (1), the first and third pairs of which are based on Isaiah 58.8–10 (in a 'Christianized' form) and 1 Corinthians 15.52f. respectively. Two collects are provided (2). The first, written by Janet Morley, has been borrowed from the Franciscan *Celebrating Common Prayer* (1992). The second was composed by the Liturgical Sub-Committee. Both prayers take account of the grief and shock with which the news of death is naturally received and emphasize the love and grace of God.

Although suggestions are made as to appropriate Psalms (4) and Scripture readings (5), no texts are printed. This is the only service in 'Funeral and Related Services' where this is the case and it seems regrettable that those using the service, or at least the person leading it, will need to turn to another book at this point.

It is suggested (6) that memories of the person who has died may be shared. In a small group of family and friends, this could be moving and therapeutic; sensitively handled, it could also play a part when a larger congregation is gathered.

The prayer which follows (7) is an extraordinarily successful combination of elements of thanksgiving, confession and petition. It acknowledges that, even as people give thanks for the life of a departed relative or friend, happy memories are often tinged with regret

for things said or done that we regret;
for things we longed to do but never did;
longed to say, but never said.

The prayer concludes with petition for the strength and courage to 'let go' of the person who has died and to trust in God.

A prayer of commendation (8) follows. Silence after the opening sentence, commending the dead person to God, leads to prayerful acknowledgement of the way in which God transforms 'the darkness of death into the dawn of new life' and of Christ's saving work. These thoughts lead naturally to a petition that all present may come to share in the joys of heaven. This prayer is adapted from a text in *Celebrating Common Prayer*, based on an earlier version in the Canadian publication *The Book of Alternative Services* (1985).

After the Lord's Prayer (9), there is a choice of texts. 'Magnified and Sanctified' (10A) is probably among the oldest prayers in *The Methodist Worship Book*. It is a translation of the Jewish *Qaddish yᵉhe shᵉlama*, which may possibly predate the Christian era. This text is used in Jewish funeral liturgies and repeated daily by relatives for 11 months after a death, and then annually on the anniversary of the death. It has been suggested that in the Lord's Prayer, with its references to hallowing God's name, to God's will and the coming of his kingdom, and to his power and glory, Jesus himself was echoing *Qaddish yᵉhe shᵉlama*. But the date of the latter is uncertain, and it is conceivable that the influence was in the opposite direction, or that both Jesus and *Qaddish* were indebted to a common source. The translation printed in *The Methodist Worship Book* is 'borrowed' from *Celebrating Common Prayer* (1992), little altered from the form in which it appeared in *The Authorised Daily Prayer Book of the United Hebrew Congregations of the British Empire* (1890).

To many people, perhaps, the language and style of *Qaddish* will seem rather strange, but its previous unfamiliarity among Methodists ought not to prevent the use of a text which, in its unremitting God-centredness, sets human life and death within the context of God's glorious and eternal being.

The alternative (10B) is an ascription of glory, an abridged version of the last two verses of the Letter of Jude. Once again, the service closes with the blessing (11) based on Philippians 4.7.

A Vigil

In some cultural traditions, it is customary for the body of a person who has died to be taken into church on the day before the funeral, and for suitable prayers to be said. Even when the body is not taken to the church, a short act of worship on the eve of the funeral – in a home, a church, or a chapel of rest – is considered appropriate. Vigils of this sort are new to British Methodist liturgical books, though for several years in some places requests have been made that ministers should lead such services. *The Methodist Worship Book* is meeting an expressed need by including 'A Vigil'.

The opening sentence (1), which faintly resembles the *Qaddish* (see above), leads to an invitation to silent prayer and remembrance of the person who has died. Silence is followed by a prayer (2), newly composed, which begins by addressing God as the one whose love embraces all his children 'in this world and the next' (an allusion to the well-known hymn 'Now thank we all our God'). It then echoes some of the confident words of Romans 8.38f., and goes on to ask that the worshippers may be united with God and with those whom they love, especially the one who has died.

The Ministry of the Word offers three passages of Scripture, one or more of which may be read, followed by a time of silence. Though, for the reasons given in Chapter Four, it is not usual for Psalms to be suggested as readings in *The Methodist Worship Book*, the first passage consists of verses from Psalm 27. Ideally, if the congregation has copies, this should be read by all, even though this is not indicated by the use of bold type.

A short litany (4) follows. Five times, an address to Christ (for example, 'Crucified Saviour'; 'Gentle Shepherd') introduces a suitable petition ('save us from the fear of death'; 'bring rest to our souls') and a version of *Kyrie eleison*. This is a beautiful prayer, full of potent biblical imagery, deeply moving in its stark simplicity.

After the Lord's Prayer (5), all present may say, as a prayer (6A), a section of the hymn popularly known as 'St Patrick's Breastplate' (see *Hymns & Psalms* 695). This is an excerpt from C.F. Alexander's translation of an Irish poem, frequently attributed to the patron saint of Ireland, who died around AD 460, although it has not been found in manuscripts older than the eleventh century. Whether or not it was written by St Patrick, it is certainly a venerable text; and this extract from it, which speaks of the all-encompassing, all-pervading presence of Christ, makes a suitable prayer at this point in 'A Vigil'. An alternative (6B) is provided – a modern composition to which the Liturgical Sub-Committee and the Faith and Order Committee should have given closer attention, for though the prayer is addressed to Jesus Christ, it concludes with the words 'In Christ's name we ask it'! This is the only place in *The Methodist Worship Book* where such an error occurs. It would have been much better if the prayer had been addressed to God the Father, 'whose Son Jesus Christ willingly gave himself up to death . . .', and on occasions when only the leader is using the book, it would be sensible to make this alteration.

The service concludes with either the Grace (7A), said by all, or the familiar blessing from Philippians 4.7 (7B). As has already been suggested (see p. 100 above), it is usually more appropriate for the Grace to be used as a greeting rather than as the conclu-sion to an act of worship. This is the second instance (the first being the provision of a Psalm as a reading) where this service breaks one of *The Methodist Worship Book*'s general rules.

Two Funeral Services

In Britain, for many centuries, the traditional pattern for a funeral service was a service in church, followed by burial in a cemetery. When crematoria were first established in the twenti-eth century, a church service before burial or cremation at first continued to be usual. It soon became common, however, for the whole service to take place at a cemetery or crematorium, espe-cially when the person who had died had no active association with a local church.

In recent years, a different pattern has developed, whereby burial or cremation takes place first, with a suitable service at the place of committal, followed by a further service in a church, either on the same day or on a subsequent day. No explanation for this alternative pattern is offered in the Introduction (p. 433), but its advocates claim that it has certain advantages over the traditional order. First, it prevents the committal from being something of an anti-climax to the proceedings (which can appear to be the case when, for example, the funeral party is obliged to drive 20 or 30 miles to a crematorium for a committal service lasting no more than five minutes, or when only a small number of those present at the church service go on to the crematorium or cemetery). Second, it allows the 'parting' to take place first, at the place of committal, so that the climax of the occasion is reached in an act of thanksgiving. A third, largely practical but not unimportant consideration is that, if there are to be refreshments, these can immediately follow the service in church, whereas when the traditional pattern is followed, most of those present at the church are likely to have left by the time that those who have gone on to the crematorium or cemetery have returned. The alternative pattern is most likely to commend itself to families with a strong connection to a local church, though even among them it has yet to establish itself as normative. It may be that, within the lifetime of *The Methodist Worship Book*, it will do so.

A Funeral Service in a Church, a Crematorium, or a Cemetery, leading to Committal

The traditional order of service has the following structure:

GATHERING
Sentences
Hymn
Prayer

THE MINISTRY OF THE WORD
Introduction
Psalm(s)
Reading(s) from the Gospels
Other Scripture reading(s)
Sermon

RESPONSE
Prayers of thanksgiving
Hymn

COMMENDATION
Prayer of commendation
The Lord's Prayer
(Blessing)
(Sentence)

COMMITTAL
Prayer of committal
Prayers
Blessing

The service begins with sentences (1), drawn from John 11.25f., which featured in the medieval Sarum rite, and which Thomas Cranmer used as the opening sentences to the 1549 burial service. These sentences are said at the entrance to the church (or crematorium or cemetery chapel) or at the graveside. One or more of a selection of additional sentences (2) may also be said, as the minister goes before the body to the front of the church, crematorium or chapel.

Two texts are offered for the prayer of approach (4), the second of which is an original composition, though the first (4A) seems to have borrowed some phrases from the equivalent prayers in *The Methodist Service Book* and others from *A New Zealand Prayer Book* (1989). The older Methodist book also provided the basis for the Introduction to the Ministry of the Word (5). Though this has been substantially rewritten, it remains a powerful and succinct statement of the Christian hope which can provide sustenance and strength in the presence of death. These words are not only an effective introduction to the Psalms and readings which follow; they also set the tone for the whole service.

One of the three Psalms (6) printed, or another Psalm (13 other possibilities are noted on p. 501), follows. In this section of the book, Psalms are not printed in bold type, perhaps because at many funerals only the minister will be handling a copy of *The Methodist Worship Book*, but, if the congregation can be supplied with copies, it is preferable for the Psalm to be said by all. The use of Psalm 23 at funerals can be traced back to the fourth century, though it did not appear in funeral liturgies standing in the tradition of *The Book of Common Prayer* until 1928. Both Psalm 130 and the verses from Psalm 103 appeared, like Psalm 23, in *The Methodist Service Book*.

Next comes a Gospel reading (7), selected from the two passages printed or from three others noted on p. 501. Surprisingly, John 14.1–6, 27 has not had a long association with funeral liturgies, though it was included in *The Book of Offices* (1936) and retained in *The Methodist Service Book*; but John 6.35–40 was included in the 1549 version of *The Book of Common Prayer*. There may be a further Bible reading (8), or more than one, for which four passages are printed and many more are suggested on pp. 501f. 1 Corinthians 15 is a traditional source of funeral readings; *The Book of Common Prayer* (1662) includes verses 20–58, which today would be thought far too long a passage. *The Methodist Service Book* offered a severely 'filleted' version of the whole chapter. *The Methodist Worship Book* prints two short extracts, together with 1 Peter 1.3–9, and a selection of verses from Romans 8, both of which appeared in the previous book.

It is appropriate that there should be a sermon (9). This should not simply be a eulogy – a tribute to the person who has died – although it is clearly desirable that there should be appropriate reference to his or her life. But the sermon is also an opportunity for the proclamation of the Christian gospel of life and hope, with its promise of consolation to those who mourn. The present book is more confident at this point than its predecessor, which indicated only that 'a sermon may be preached'. The rubric in *The Methodist Worship Book* is not permissive.

The Response begins with thanksgiving (10), expressed in two prayers, based on texts from *The Methodist Service Book*. The first gives thanks for the saving work of God in Christ. The second is both a thanksgiving for the life of the person who has died and for his or her release from the tribulations of this world, and a petition that the worshippers may be brought with him or her to the joy of God's perfect kingdom. It is interesting to note that the opportunity has been taken, in the revision of this second prayer, to refer directly to the person who has died, whereas, in its original form, it referred throughout to God's 'departed servants' and did not become specific at any point.

When *The Methodist Service Book* appeared, the provision of an act of Commendation, distinct from the Committal, was a relatively new idea to churches influenced by the Prayer Book tradition. The editors were no doubt influenced by similar provision in the Church of England's 1965 'Series 2' burial service. It is indeed helpful to distinguish the commendation of the whole person to the mercy of God from the committal of the body to the ground or the elements.

The first form of the Commendation (12A) is used in funeral liturgies in many parts of the world. This was the only form of Commendation included in the draft edition of *The Methodist Worship Book*, but the Conference Revision Committee accepted a proposal that the second form (12B), a shortened form of the Commendation from the previous service book, should be given as an alternative. Whichever form is used, the Lord's Prayer (13) follows.

If the whole service is taking place in a crematorium chapel or at the graveside, it proceeds immediately to the Committal (17). If, however, the service has begun in church or in a cemetery chapel, the usual blessing (15), from Philippians 4.7, draws this part of the service to a close, and the Committal is preceded, during the procession into the crematorium or to the grave, by one or more Scripture sentences (16).

Two different forms of the Committal (17) are provided; circumstances will determine which one is more appropriate for use in any given case. The central section of each, 'we commit *her/his* body . . . earth to earth, ashes to ashes, dust to dust, in sure and certain hope . . .', is part of Cranmer's revision (in 1549 and 1552) of the medieval Sarum rite's Committal. The Committal may be followed (18) by a 'filleted' version of Revelation 14.13, a verse whose use after the Committal can also be traced back to Cranmer. In the present book, it does not begin with 'I heard a voice from heaven, saying . . .', as it did in *The Methodist Service Book*. There was anecdotal evidence to suggest that this introduction to the crucial words of the verse was sometimes confusing to those hearing it, since it was not always obvious to them that it was a quotation from Scripture, rather than the minister's personal testimony!

Five prayers (19), one or more of which may be said, draw the service towards its conclusion. Three of these previously appeared in *The Methodist Service Book*: the first (19A), 'Father of all . . .', incorporates phrases from the traditional Requiem Mass, its original inspiration being 2 Esdras 2.34f. Its inclusion in 1975 was slightly controversial, though it was not challenged in 1998. It is, after all, an optional prayer, and, while some regard any sort of prayer for the departed to be theologically indefensible, others believe that it is entirely natural to wish to pray for the person who has died, as well as for the bereaved.

The second prayer carried over from *The Methodist Service Book*, 'Father of mercies . . .' (19B), is a revised version of a prayer in the 1940 edition of the Scottish *Book of Common Order*. It is a petition for the comfort of those who mourn and its first line is a quotation from 2 Corinthians 1.3. The third prayer, 'Grant us, O God . . .' (19C), is adapted from Frank Colquhoun's *Parish Prayers* (1964); some of its phrases have been attributed to St Augustine of Hippo. This is a prayer for the strengthening and sustaining of the mourners.

Two new prayers have found their way into this section, though they are new only in the sense that they have not previously appeared in Methodist books. The beautiful 'Support us, O Lord . . .' (19D) is of uncertain origin, though it has been attributed to the Elizabethan era, and was known to John Henry Newman, who quoted it in one of his published *Sermons*. The equally lovely prayer, 'Bring us, Lord our God . . .' (19E), is based on a section of a sermon, preached in 1627 or 1628, by the priest and poet John Donne. These two additions to the post-

Committal prayers are not only aesthetically appealing; they breathe a serenity, a sense of calm and peace in God's eternal presence, which can contribute much to the service at this point.

The Blessing (20) with which the service concludes may be in one of two forms. The first (20A) is an amended version of a text from *A New Zealand Prayer Book* (1989). The second (20B), a shorter version of which appeared as a prayer in *The Methodist Service Book*, is derived from the Church of England's 1971 report, *Prayer and the Departed*.

A Funeral Service at a Crematorium or Cemetery, followed by a Service of Thanksgiving in Church

The structure of the second funeral service is as follows:

AT THE CREMATORIUM OR CEMETERY

GATHERING

Sentences
Hymn
Prayer

THE MINISTRY OF THE WORD

Introduction
Psalm(s)
Reading(s) from the Gospels
Other Scripture reading(s)
Short address or reflection

COMMENDATION

Prayer of thanksgiving
Prayer of commendation

COMMITTAL

Prayer of committal
Sentence
Prayers

The Lord's Prayer
Blessing

AT THE CHURCH

GATHERING

Sentence
Hymn
Prayer

THE MINISTRY OF THE WORD

Introduction
Psalm
Other Scripture reading(s)
Sermon
Hymn

RESPONSE

Prayers
The Lord's Prayer
Hymn
Blessing

It will be noted that the first part of the service, at the crematorium or cemetery, has a structure almost identical to that of the traditional service. Most of the printed texts are also common to both services, and do not, therefore, require any further commentary here. One exception occurs in the opening prayers, where the first (4A) is different from its equivalent in the traditionally-structured service. It is a revised version of the second prayer of approach in the funeral service from *The Methodist Service Book*. There is also a slightly different selection of Scripture sentences (2), for reasons which are not entirely clear.

Instead of a sermon, as in the first service, there is provision (9) for 'a short address or reflection'. This is because the sermon will be preached during the subsequent Service of Thanksgiving, rather than at the place of committal.

In the second service, the Commendation begins (10) with a prayer of thanksgiving (for the life of the departed person and for the gospel of life and hope). This is not the text used in the first service, though it occupies a roughly equivalent place.

The Philippians blessing (18A) replaces the first form of the blessing used in the traditional service, for this text will appear later, at the end of the Service of Thanksgiving (31A).

At the church, there is provision (20) for the Service of Thanksgiving to begin with the placing of an urn or casket containing ashes on a table in front of the communion table. This will not happen, of course, if the second part of the service immediately follows the first, and may not happen in any case. Provision is made for it, for those occasions when the second part of the service happens at a later date and when the presence of the ashes is desired by the family of the person who has died.

The sentences (21) are from 1 Peter 1.3f. Surprisingly, when one considers their obvious appropriateness, they have not traditionally been included in funeral liturgies and they are used nowhere else among the 'Funeral and Related Services'. This is one of the few instances of *The Methodist Worship Book* printing *The Revised English Bible*'s translation rather than that of *The New Revised Standard Version* (though 'Praise be to' has been substituted for 'Praised be' in the first sentence).

The first of the two prayers of approach (23A) is from *Celebrating Common Prayer* (1992). It illustrates the way in which some prayers can be adapted to varying contexts; in *Celebrating Common Prayer* it is the opening prayer in the office for Saturday morning, and has no association whatsoever with funerals. The second prayer (23B) is one of the collects for Easter Day; its use in the present context is a powerful reminder that the Christian hope of life beyond death is grounded in the resurrection of Christ. This theme is also reflected in the introduction to the Ministry of the Word (24).

There is provision for a Psalm and Scripture readings (25), though no texts are printed. The list on pp. 501f. supplies an abundance of suitable passages. A sermon (26) follows.

The Response begins with an act of praise (28) in the form of the middle section of *Te Deum Laudamus* (see above, p. 44). The use of these verses in the context of a funeral service was pioneered by *The Alternative Service Book* (1980).

It might have been expected that a new section number would introduce the prayers which follow, but that is not the case. This very minor sin of omission is unlikely to be noticed by many worshippers, as the prayers proceed with a carefully composed mixture of thanksgiving and intercession, during which there is an opportunity for members of the congregation to pray in silence, or aloud, in reference to the person for whose life thanksgiving is being offered. These prayers very fittingly conclude with a collect which has been associated with All Saints' Day since 1549. (The same collect appears in a slightly different form on p. 558.)

A Funeral Service for a Child

In *The Methodist Service Book* it was taken for granted that the book's single service for 'The Burial or Cremation of the Dead' would be used for the funeral of a child, though some suggestions were made for variant texts in these circumstances. The present book, by contrast, provides a full order of service for the funeral of a child, which, though it follows the basic structure of the traditional funeral service, is clearly designed for these particularly tragic circumstances.

The Scripture sentences (1) include some which refer directly to children. It would obviously be appropriate for at least one of these to be read. A gently worded sentence (2), stating the purposes for which the congregation has gathered, precedes the prayers of approach (3), which begin with an invitation to pray in silence. There is recognition at this point of the 'confusion and sorrow . . . anger and pain', which are felt in such circumstances. It is very important that these feelings should be acknowledged. After the silence, one of two prayers is said. 4A is a simplified form of the first prayer in the funeral service in *The Methodist Service Book*, and is not used elsewhere in *The Methodist Wor-*

ship Book. 4B is adapted from a prayer in *The Alternative Service Book* (1980).

For the Ministry of the Word, one Psalm and three Scripture readings are printed (5); one or more of these may be read, or some other passage or passages may be selected. Considerable flexibility is desirable at this point, in order that the pastoral needs of those present may be met as fully as possible. Difficult though this may sometimes be, it is right that a sermon (6) should be preached: the Gospel's message of comfort and hope needs to be expounded in these sad circumstances.

The need for adaptability is also recognized in the rubric (7) which introduces the prayer with which the Commendation starts. Not every phrase in this lovely prayer will be appropriate in every case. The two forms of the prayer of commendation itself (8) are identical to those in the two previous funeral services, and the usual blessing (Philippians 4.7) is said if the Committal is to take place elsewhere.

When this is the case, the minister says one or more of the three Scripture sentences (11) prior to the Committal. The second of these is also printed among the opening sentences (1) and should not be repeated at this point if it has been said earlier. The first sentence of the Committal (12) is based on a prayer from *The Methodist Service Book*, used in *The Methodist Worship Book* only here and in the service which follows; its original source is the Scottish *Book of Common Order* (1940). Its confident assertion that God has made nothing in vain and loves all that he has made is very appropriate in this context. Silence (13) follows the Committal.

The prayers for the bereaved (15) are designed either to be used in full or to be adapted as may seem appropriate. Largely based on incidents recorded in the Gospels, these prayers sensitively relate God's love and compassion, revealed in the Scriptures, to the circumstances of those who now mourn the loss of a child. There is provision for some other prayer to be said instead.

One or more further prayers (16) may also be said, though this will rarely be necessary if the printed prayers for the bereaved

(15) have been used. The second (16B) is adapted from *The Book of Alternative Services* (1985). After the Lord's Prayer (17), the extract from 'St Patrick's Breastplate' (see above, p. 167) is said (18). Either the Aaronic Blessing (19A), whose association with Baptism gives its use here a special resonance, or a blessing (19B) from *A New Zealand Prayer Book* (1989) brings the service to a close.

A Funeral Service for a Stillborn Child

The Methodist Service Book made no special provision for the funeral of a stillborn child, but, following many requests, the Faith and Order Committee produced a form of service for this purpose, which was adopted by the Conference in 1984. The pastoral need for an appropriate and significant liturgical act following a stillbirth (or a miscarriage, or a neo-natal death, for which this service can be adapted) has been widely recognized in recent years. The Notes (p. 489) suggest that the circumstances in which this service may be used will vary considerably. Great sensitivity is needed by those who lead it.

The opening sentences (1), unusually, are not from Scripture. They seek to set the pain and sorrow of the bereaved in the context of God's love and grace. Silent prayer (2) leads to a short prayer of approach. Either Psalm 23 or Psalm 139.1, 13–18 may be read (3). The latter is used nowhere else in this section of the book, despite a long association with funeral liturgies, but it has powerful resonances in this context, so powerful indeed that ministers may sometimes judge that the bereaved persons would not be able to bear its use. Where this is the case, it would be much better to read the familiar words of Psalm 23.

Three Scripture readings (4) are printed, which focus respectively on the place of children in the kingdom of heaven, Christ's invitation to those who are burdened, and the God of all consolation; one or more of these, or some other passage(s), may be read. There is a short address or reflection (5), rather than a sermon.

As the service moves towards the Commendation, a short prayer of thanksgiving (6) recognizes that the one whose loss is being mourned is, like those who mourn, an heir to God's promises. The Commendation itself (7) is very brief; it is in essence the second and shorter Commendation included in the first two funeral services.

If there is to be a Committal which will take place elsewhere, the Grace (9) is said before departure and a Scripture sentence, or more than one (10), upon arrival at the place of committal. The Committal prayer used in 'A Funeral Service for a Child' is also used here (11).

Four short prayers follow (12), which may be used as appropriate. The first three were newly composed for *The Methodist Worship Book*. The fourth is the Frank Colquhoun prayer (see above, p. 173). Once again, the need for sensitivity in choosing which, if any, of these prayers should be said must be emphasized. The Lord's Prayer (13) leads to the Blessing, which is either the Philippians text (13A) or (13B) the second Blessing from 'A Funeral Service for a Child' (see p. 179 above).

A Service for the Burial of Ashes

From the time of the publication of *The Methodist Service Book*, many requests were made for the provision of a service for the burial or scattering of ashes. Many people wish the cremated remains of their loved ones to be interred or scattered in a liturgical act, and this service is designed for that purpose. It is a short service which takes care not to repeat anything that has already been said or done in the funeral service (apart from the Lord's Prayer, which is used in virtually every act of Christian worship, and one other prayer, discussed below).

After the people have gathered at the place of burial (or scattering) (1), the minister's opening words (2) are a call to remember that 'although our bodies return to dust, we shall be raised with Christ in glory'. The passages suggested for the Ministry of the Word (3) are extremely brief, each consisting of one or, at the most, two sentences, though other passages could be substituted or added. The prayer which follows takes its first sentence from 'An Office of Commendation' (p. 439), but continues differently, with the first hint that this service is an important transitional moment in the process of 'letting go': 'lift us from the darkness of grief into the light of your presence'. This note will be sounded again.

Commendation and Committal have, of course, already taken place at the funeral, so the words spoken as the ashes are lowered into the ground (5) refer to what has previously happened and indicate what is taking place now. Of the three prayers (6), one or more of which may next be said, the first (6A) is the only text, apart from the Lord's Prayer, which is printed both in the funeral services and in this service. It is the splendid prayer for 'those whom we love but see no longer', derived from *The Methodist Service Book*, and discussed above (p. 173). The second is a new composition, and the third is a much-amended version of a prayer from the Australian book *Uniting in Worship* (1988).

Whichever form of the Dismissal and Blessing (8) is used, though especially when it is the first (8A), the concept of going forward from the present moment to continue the earthly journey is expressed. This picks up the idea that this service is, when it is used, the final liturgical act in the process of the 'letting go' of a loved one. This is not to suggest that the sense of loss and the grief which accompany bereavement will no longer be experienced, but the service should mark a significant stage in the process of readjustment.

So ends the third-longest section of *The Methodist Worship Book*, which, in its abundant provision of liturgical material for use before, at, and after funerals, is, for Methodists, an unprecedentedly rich pastoral resource.

17

Blessing and Dedication Services

This short section is another of the innovations in *The Methodist Worship Book*, no similar liturgies having appeared in previous Methodist service books. The first service was supplied in recognition of the fact that ministers and others occasionally (indeed frequently in some places) receive requests for the blessing of a home. The other services are liturgies for the laying of a foundation stone and the dedication of church buildings, occasions for which ministers have often had to devise their own services in the absence of published liturgies of good quality.

These services are unique in that their first drafts were produced, not by members of the Liturgical Sub-Committee, but by Dr (now Professor) Susan White, a distinguished American liturgiologist. Although Professor White's material was considerably reshaped, her contribution gave this part of the book a style somewhat different from the rest.

An Order for the Blessing of a Home

When all who are to share in this service have assembled at the home (1), the person leading the service says a sentence (2) based on 1 Samuel 25.6 and Luke 10.5. The prayer of invocation (3) which follows combines the idea of God making a home in the human heart with prayer for those who make their home in the place where the service is being held.

One of two familiar Psalms (Psalms 23 and 95.1–7) may be read or sung (4). It seems unlikely that the Psalm will often be sung in a prose setting (for example, to an 'Anglican chant'), but of course one of the many metrical versions of Psalm 23 may be sung and there is a metrical version of Psalm 95 in *Hymns &* *Psalms* (no. 567).

The suggested Scripture passages (5), one or more of which may be read, cover a wide range of ideas. The appropriateness to this occasion of some of the passages is less obvious than that of others, and care needs to be taken over the selection.

A set of prayers (6) for the home and those who live there is followed by the Lord's Prayer (7). Before the Grace (9) brings this short service to a close, there is provision (8) for the inclusion of a symbolic act, several suggestions being made about the form that this might take. Clearly it will normally be necessary to discuss in advance with the person or persons whose home is to be blessed whether any such act should take place and, if so, what it should be. For the leader to go out into the garden at this point and plant a tree, without previous consultation, would be highly undesirable!

The content of this service is such that, if necessary, it can easily be used when only the leader has a copy of the book. The response included in the prayers is familiar to most Methodists (and easily learned by those to whom it is not); the Lord's Prayer and the Grace are also texts which many people can say from memory.

An Order for the Laying of a Foundation Stone

Note 1 (p. 507) could scarcely have been written some years ago, and some readers may not be entirely happy with it even now. It envisages that, when a foundation stone is to be laid, not only should Christians of other local churches and representatives of wider Methodism be invited, but also representatives of 'other religious traditions'. This reflects a growing consciousness of the multi-faith character of modern Britain and of the need for the various faith communities to understand one another, and to work together and extend hospitality to one another wherever possible. The concept of 'sacred space' is common to most of the world's religions and, of all the services in the book, this is the one which would be the easiest for people of other faiths to attend. Clearly, however, local circumstances will vary and these will help to determine what is appropriate.

The assumption is that a stone-laying ceremony will normally take place in relation to a place of worship, but Note 2 indicates that adaptations to the service will need to be made in other circumstances.

The order begins with the Grace (1), here used, as is normally the case in *The Methodist Worship Book*, as a greeting. An informal welcome (2) leads to words of introduction (3), briefly explaining the circumstances that have led up to the present moment. Then at least one passage of Scripture, selected from the six suggested (4), is read.

The rubric (5) which indicates that a sermon may be preached may seem surprising, since such ceremonies take place out of doors and are usually brief. It is for this reason that the rubric is permissive; on a cold winter morning, a sermon may not seem desirable; on a warm and bright summer afternoon, matters might appear different. In any event, however, a sermon on such an occasion should be short and to the point.

The foundation stone is laid by the appointed person (6), who says a suitable sentence, and then the minister offers prayer (7) for God's blessing upon the building project and upon the church community. The Lord's Prayer (8) is said.

The congregation next joins in an act of commitment (9) which concludes with responsive sentences, the first pair of which, appropriately enough, are based on David's prayer (1 Chronicles 29.11, 14) when gifts had been assembled for the proposed temple in Jerusalem. The service ends with a blessing (10) and a dismissal (11).

An Order for the Dedication of a Church Building and its Furnishings

Note 1 (p. 510) points out that it is desirable that a building should be set apart for holy use in a service during which the word of God is proclaimed and the Lord's Supper is celebrated. The Note goes on to acknowledge that it will not always seem practicable to include the Eucharist in such a dedication service (perhaps because of the likely presence of a number of people who are not communicants), and indicates that in such circumstances the Lord's Supper should, if possible, be celebrated on the following Sunday.

Note 2 envisages the possibility of a procession from another place to the building which is to be dedicated. It is suggested that, whether or not this is to happen, some or all of the congregation may assemble at the church door for the first part of the service. Such ritual movement can effectively mark the 'entering into' a new beginning for the local Christian community, and it is indeed often the case that new premises provide new impetus for worship, mission and service.

Psalm 100 may be said responsively at the church door (1); its reference to coming into God's courts with thanksgiving makes it ideal for such an occasion. A simple sentence (2) stating the purpose of the service is followed by a short collect (3) which includes an evocative reference to Jacob's response to his dream at Bethel (Genesis 28.17).

The rest of the service falls into four or five principal sections:

The Presentation
The Ministry of the Word
The Dedication
(The Lord's Supper, or a prayer of thanksgiving)
Blessing and Dismissal.

The Presentation begins (4) when a person involved with the planning, construction or furnishing of the new building hands a key to a representative of the local church. It is good that there should be liturgical recognition of the role that architects, quantity surveyors, builders and others have played in bringing the building project to completion; the person handing over the key is a representative of them all. The local church's representative replies appropriately, and then the presiding minister may invite the local minister or some other person to say by what name the church is to be called. It could be thought that the question and answer are rather 'high flown', and in truth there may be circumstances (for instance when a new building has replaced one which has stood on the same site for 200 years and when no change of name is involved) in which they would be better omitted. But names are important in many ways and, especially if the building is on a new site, this 'naming ceremony' can help to establish identity.

The presiding minister then calls for the doors to be opened (5) and prays that Christ's love may dwell in the building and that all who enter may find peace. Any who have assembled outside or at the door take their places inside the building (6).

The Ministry of the Word follows its normal pattern, with Old Testament reading (7), Psalm (8), Epistle (9), Gospel (11) and sermon (12). No fewer than 17 passages are suggested as possibilities for the readings and Psalm and it should not be difficult to make an appropriate selection from these.

The Dedication begins with a prayer for God's blessing, followed by a dedication of the church building in the Names of the Persons of the Trinity and a dedication of those present (14). A number of striking images are included in the prayer (for example, 'a fortress against all hatred' and 'a beacon to all who seek your presence').

Prayers are then said (15) at the font or baptistry, at the pulpit or reading desk, and at the communion table. These features of the church building have, of course, a practical purpose; they are there to be used. But they are also permanent symbols (or should be) of the purposes for which they are used. Taken together, they symbolize the proclamation of God's Word and the celebration of the sacraments, which are at the heart of Christian worship.

It may be desirable to offer further prayers in respect of musical instruments or other furnishings, and provision is made for this (16). Then comes a litany (17), the first section of which echoes Solomon's prayer at the Dedication of the Temple (2 Chronicles 6) by beginning petition after petition with the word 'When', and in the versicle and response ('Lord, have mercy. **Lord, hear us**'), which may be compared with 2 Chronicles 6.30. After a silence, the litany draws towards its close with prayer addressed to each Person of the Trinity, and then concludes with the only prayer in this service, apart from the Lord's Prayer (18), which has not been newly composed. This concluding collect is ancient; it appeared in the Gregorian Sacramentary and in *The Book of Common Prayer* (1662). The prayer is also unusual in deviating in the first part of its structure from the conventional collect form, which is discussed on p. 520 of *The Methodist Worship Book*.

'Holy Communion for Pentecost and Times of Renewal in the Life of the Church' is recommended for use (19) if the Lord's Supper is to be celebrated. Otherwise, a short prayer of thanksgiving (20) is said, prior to the blessing and dismissal (22), which, unusually, are not numbered separately.

18

Calendar, Collects and Lectionary

The Introduction (pp. 519ff.) to the final, and second-longest, section of *The Methodist Worship Book* helpfully discusses the traditional pattern of the Christian year, the use of liturgical colours, the characteristics of collects and of the lectionaries used in the book, and the steps that need to be taken to identify the appropriate collect and readings for any given date. The table of moveable dates on p. 522 is an invaluable aid to the latter process.

One of the achievements of *The Methodist Service Book*, in the years following its publication in 1975, was the way in which it made Methodists more aware than they had previously been of the onward march of the Christian year and the value of lectionaries in providing a systematic coverage of Scripture over a period of years. The Calendar which was incorporated into *The Methodist Service Book* was strongly influenced by the proposals of the ecumenical body, the Joint Liturgical Group, whose related collects and Lectionary were also used. The latter will be discussed later in this chapter.

The Calendar

The Christian Calendar evolved slowly over the early centuries of the Church's existence, but its general shape has changed little in the last 1,000 years. That shape is described on p. 519 of *The Methodist Worship Book*.

The Joint Liturgical Group's Calendar, used in *The Methodist Service Book*, introduced a number of modifications to the traditional shape (such as the provision of nine Sundays before Christmas and nine before Easter, thus in effect extending Advent and Lent), which were widely adopted by British churches at that time. Most churches, however, in their most recent Calendars, have reverted to the traditional pattern, though there is some variation in the naming of Sundays.

A brief explanation of some of the names used by *The Methodist Worship Book* may be helpful. First, the fact that the season of Christmas extends for twelve days and always includes at least one Sunday (there may be two) is recognized by the designations 'The First Sunday of Christmas' and 'The Second Sunday of Christmas'. To refer to these Sundays as Sundays 'after' Christmas would have been to reinforce the unfortunate, but widespread, notion that Christmas ends on Christmas Day – the day on which it begins!

For similar reasons, *The Methodist Worship Book* refers to Sundays 'of' rather than Sundays 'after' Easter.

Ordinary Time, sometimes described as 'Ordinary Seasons' in *The Methodist Worship Book*, consists of those parts of the year which do not belong to either of the two great cycles. The Christmas cycle centres on the incarnation; it has a preparatory period, Advent, and extends beyond Christmas Day to the Epiphany. The Easter cycle centres on Christ's death and resurrection; it begins with Lent and Passiontide and extends through the great Fifty Days of Easter to the Day of Pentecost. So Ordinary Time also comes in two blocks – a short one, between the Sunday after Epiphany and Ash Wednesday, and a long one, which follows the Day of Pentecost and precedes Advent. In order to make it as easy as possible for users to identify the correct Sunday during Ordinary Time, *The Methodist Worship Book* indicates the dates between which a particular Sunday may fall (for example, 'Sunday between 23 and 29 October inclusive – Thirtieth Sunday in Ordinary Time').

The larger, second block of Ordinary Time has been variously designated. A long English tradition, originating in the medieval Sarum Calendar, referred to this period as 'Sundays after Trinity'. The Joint Liturgical Group proposed that all these

Sundays should be designated 'Sundays after Pentecost' and this proposal was adopted in *The Methodist Service Book* (1975) and *The Alternative Service Book* (1980). Oddly, however, since the word 'after' was used, rather than 'in', this designation gave rise to the mistaken idea that there was a season of Pentecost, which had its own character in the way of Easter and Christmas. In *Common Worship* (2000), the Church of England has restored 'Sundays after Trinity' in its designation of collects, though in the Lectionary it refers to 'proper' Sundays and assigns dates to them (for example, Proper 21 – Sunday between 25 September and 1 October). *The Methodist Worship Book* refers to 'Sundays in Ordinary Time', numbering those after Pentecost consecutively to those before Lent.

It ought to be mentioned that the traditional Calendar has two parts, one of which is included in *The Methodist Worship Book* but the other of which is represented only in a vestigial way. The part of the Calendar familiar to Methodists, which stretches from Advent, through Christmas, Lent, Easter, Pentecost and Trinity, to Ordinary Time, is what is known as the *Temporale*. The other part of the traditional Calendar, the *Sanctorale*, has not appeared in any significant way in any Methodist service book; it is the calendar of saints' days and other similar commemorations. The only traces of the *Sanctorale* in *The Methodist Worship Book* are the provision of readings and collects for use on All Saints' Day and others for Wesley Day or Aldersgate Sunday! Methodists who wish to observe 'St Joseph of Nazareth' or 'The Birth of the Blessed Virgin Mary' will need to look elsewhere for readings and collects.

Liturgical Colours

The changing moods of the Christian year can be represented visually by the use of liturgical colours, which are now much more widely employed in Methodism than was once the case. More ministers wear coloured stoles according to the season or special day and more churches have furnishings, such as pulpit falls, which are changed on the same basis. On those pages in which the Calendar and Lectionary appear (pp. 566–600), guidance is given about what colour is appropriate for each Sunday or other occasion.

The Collects

Nothing needs to be added to the account which the Introduction (p. 520) gives of the traditional purpose and shape of the collect, though in the following pages an attempt will be made to identify the sources of the collects which are included in the book and occasionally to comment on their content.

The numbered acknowledgements which accompany the collects on pp. 523–63 (the 'key' to which is found on pp. 604f.) indicate only the source from which the compilers of *The Methodist Worship Book* directly 'borrowed'. They do not necessarily reveal the original source. This may be illustrated by reference to the Second Collect for Christmas Eve, which is attributed to *The Alternative Service Book* (1980), hiding the fact that the collect appeared in the Gelasian Sacramentary, the Gregorian Sacramentary, the Sarum Missal and the Prayer Books of 1549 and 1928. Clearly, such detail could not be included in the Acknowledgements, but the following notes will attempt to trace sources with greater thoroughness.

There will be frequent references to the Leonine, Gelasian and Gregorian Sacramentaries, to the Sarum Missal and to various editions of *The Book of Common Prayer*. These important sources have been discussed in Chapter Four (pp. 37–40 above).

One further point needs to be made before the individual collects are considered. A serious effort was made by the major British churches during the 1970s to reach a common mind about collects and, if possible, to adopt an identical scheme for their use. Work was carried out to some extent independently, for example by the Church of England's Liturgical Commission, which published *Collects to Accompany the Lectionary for Holy Communion Series 3* in 1975. In the same year, *The Methodist*

Service Book contained almost exactly the same selection of collects, with very few textual variations. Both churches were drawing very heavily on the work that was being undertaken by the Joint Liturgical Group. The Group had published a set of collects in 1968 and continued to work, in close co-operation with the appropriate bodies of its member churches, on their revision. Often, the same people would be involved in discussion of the collects in the liturgical groups of their own denominations and in the Joint Liturgical Group. This was a fine example of ecumenical co-operation, but it now makes the precise identification of the sources of some translations and some new collects which date from the 1970s virtually impossible. In the notes which follow, such collects will be attributed to the Joint Liturgical Group.

FIRST SUNDAY OF ADVENT

First Collect

Thomas Cranmer wrote this collect for *The Book of Common Prayer* (1549), drawing material for it from prayers in the Gelasian and Gregorian Sacramentaries. Part of its original inspiration is Romans 13.12.

Second Collect

This is a recent revision, by the International Commission on English in the Liturgy, of a prayer from the Gelasian Sacramentary. Both collects reflect an important and traditional Advent theme – the need for alertness and readiness for Christ's coming in glory.

SECOND SUNDAY OF ADVENT

First Collect

The first collect comes from the Australian book *Uniting in Worship* (1988).

Second Collect

This collect, composed by the International Commission on English in the Liturgy, is full of biblical allusions. Words from Psalm 8.5, Luke 1.68, 44, and Hebrews 10.23 are skilfully woven together.

THIRD SUNDAY OF ADVENT

First Collect

Though 'borrowed' in almost this form from the Canadian publication *The Book of Alternative Services* (1985), this prayer is in fact a revision of a collect written for this Sunday by John Cosin, which first appeared in *The Book of Common Prayer* (1662).

Second Collect

This collect was composed by the Liturgical Sub-Committee.

FOURTH SUNDAY OF ADVENT

First Collect

This prayer admirably illustrates the complex history which underlies so many collects. It is a revision of the Joint Liturgical Group's version of a prayer which appeared (without attribution) in Frank Colquhoun's *Parish Prayers* (1964). Different versions of it have appeared in the Joint Liturgical Group's *The Daily Office* (1968) and *The Daily Office Revised* (1978), in *The Methodist Service Book* (1975), in *The Alternative Service Book* (1980) and in *Common Worship* (2000).

Second Collect

This lovely collect is the work of the International Commission on English in the Liturgy.

CHRISTMAS EVE

First Collect

This, the shortest collect in *The Methodist Worship Book*, is taken from *A New Zealand Prayer Book* (1989).

Second Collect

As already indicated on p. 191 above, this collect has a much longer history than its attribution to *The Alternative Service Book* (1980) would suggest.

CHRISTMAS DAY (MIDNIGHT)

First Collect

The Gelasian Sacramentary assigned this collect to the Christmas Vigil Mass and it also appeared in the Gregorian Sacramentary and the Sarum Missal. It was translated from the Roman Missal by the Joint Liturgical Group in 1968 and has been widely used since then.

Second Collect

This unusual collect, by Gordon Nodwell, is from *Worship for All Seasons 1* (1993).

CHRISTMAS DAY

First Collect

Thomas Cranmer based this collect on a Christmas prayer from the Gelasian Sacramentary and included it in the 1549 Prayer Book.

Second Collect

Written by the Liturgical Sub-Committee, the second collect cites John 1.14 and makes an important (and thoroughly Johannine) connection between 'glory' and 'splendour' and 'self-giving love'.

FIRST SUNDAY OF CHRISTMAS

First Collect

This ancient collect, from the Leonine Sacramentary and the Sarum Missal, was not used by Thomas Cranmer. It appeared, however, in the 1928 proposals for the revision of *The Book of Common Prayer* and, before its inclusion in the Joint Liturgical Group's *The Daily Office Revised* (1978), it was printed in *The Methodist Service Book* (1975). *The Alternative Service Book* (1980) also used it.

Second Collect

By contrast, the second collect is a recent composition, which has been taken from *Supplemental Liturgical Resources* of the American Presbyterian Church.

SECOND SUNDAY OF CHRISTMAS

First Collect

Both collects for this Sunday are recent compositions. The first appeared in the Canadian publication *The Book of Alternative Services* (1985).

Second Collect

This collect was written by the American Lutheran Gail Ramshaw, and first published in 1988.

THE EPIPHANY

First Collect

The Book of Common Worship of the Church of South India (1963) is the original source of this collect, which was included in the Joint Liturgical Group's publications of 1968 and 1978.

Second Collect

The Uniting Church of Australia included this collect in *Uniting in Worship* (1988).

SUNDAY AFTER EPIPHANY AND FIRST SUNDAY IN ORDINARY TIME

First Collect

This collect was newly composed by the Joint Liturgical Group for *The Daily Office Revised* (1978), though it echoes some older prayers.

Second Collect

Though the immediate source of the second collect is the Church of Scotland's *Book of Common Order* (1994), an earlier version appeared in *The Daily Office Revised* (1978), which was itself inspired by a collect from the Church of South India.

SECOND SUNDAY IN ORDINARY TIME

First Collect

Having first been published in *The Book of Common Worship of the Church of South India* (1963), this collect was included by the Joint Liturgical Group in *The Daily Office* (1968) and *The Daily Office Revised* (1978).

Second Collect

The second collect is a Joint Liturgical Group composition, but it is based on a prayer from the Leonine Sacramentary. (The third collect for Ash Wednesday is a different, and older, translation of the same original Latin text.)

THIRD SUNDAY IN ORDINARY TIME

First Collect

This collect is a new composition by the Liturgical Sub-Committee, which weaves together themes from the Gospel lections, especially those of Years A and B (see *The Methodist Worship Book*, p. 521).

Second Collect

The second collect is derived from *The Daily Office Revised* (1978). It was written to reflect the theme for the Seventh Sunday before Easter in the Joint Liturgical Group's Lectionary of that time, 'Christ, Worker of Miracles'. The second part of the collect may have been influenced by the collect for the Third Sunday after Epiphany in *The Book of Common Prayer* (1662), which appears as the second collect for the Twenty-seventh Sunday in Ordinary Time in *The Methodist Worship Book*.

FOURTH SUNDAY IN ORDINARY TIME

First Collect

This collect was composed by the Liturgical Sub-Committee.

Second Collect

With 1 Corinthians 13 in mind, Thomas Cranmer composed the collect on which the present text is based in 1549.

FIFTH SUNDAY IN ORDINARY TIME

First Collect

The attribution to the Australian book *Uniting in Worship* is correct as far as it goes, but this collect is essentially a prayer of St Augustine of Hippo (AD 354–430).

Second Collect

The Canadian service book *The Book of Alternative Services* (1985) is the source of this collect.

SIXTH SUNDAY IN ORDINARY TIME

First Collect

The beauty and succinctness of this collect, one of the shortest in *The Methodist Worship Book*, make it especially memorable. It can be found in the Gelasian and Gregorian Sacramentaries, the Sarum Missal, successive versions of *The Book of Common Prayer* and almost every liturgical book influenced by the Prayer Book tradition.

Second Collect

The source of this collect is the International Commission on English in the Liturgy, whose proposals for the revision of the Roman Sacramentary include the provision of this prayer on this day.

SEVENTH SUNDAY IN ORDINARY TIME

First Collect

The first collect has come from New Zealand. Since the Gospel reading in each of the three Lectionary years is about love and forgiveness, the appropriateness of the collect is obvious.

Second Collect

This collect, from the International Commission on English in the Liturgy, has, like the first collect, been selected for this Sunday because of its appropriateness to the Gospel lections.

EIGHTH SUNDAY IN ORDINARY TIME

First Collect

The Leonine Sacramentary is the earliest known source of this collect, which was included in the Sarum Missal and successive editions of *The Book of Common Prayer* and which appeared in *The Methodist Service Book* (1975) and *The Alternative Service Book* (1980).

Second Collect

The proposals for the revision of the Roman Sacramentary, made by the International Commission on English in the Liturgy, include a version of this collect, which has been considerably revised for *The Methodist Worship Book*. The Old Testament reading for this Sunday in Year B is Hosea 2.14–20, where there are references, as in the collect, to the desert and to God's covenant love.

SUNDAY BEFORE LENT

First Collect

First composed for the Feast of the Transfiguration in the proposed revision of *The Book of Common Prayer* in 1928, this prayer has since been substantially revised by the Joint Liturgical Group (1978) and included in many subsequent service books.

Second Collect

The second collect is a fine example of the 'modern renaissance' of collects to which the Introduction (p. 520) refers. Written by

John V. Taylor, it is a highly appropriate prayer for this Sunday, when Transfiguration lections are read and Lent draws near.

Ash Wednesday

First Collect

This collect was composed by Cranmer for *The Book of Common Prayer* (1549) for use on this day and it has appeared in most service books of the Prayer Book tradition.

Second Collect

This simplified version of the first collect is from *A New Zealand Prayer Book* (1989). Cranmer's original (only slightly altered in the first form) is regarded by some as even more heavily penitential in tone ('lamenting our sins and acknowledging our wretchedness') than this day requires. Those who take that view may find the New Zealand text more palatable.

Third Collect

The third collect (supplied because the first and second are versions of the same text) is a translation of a prayer from the Leonine Sacramentary, made for the 1928 proposed revision of *The Book of Common Prayer*. (An alternative form of this prayer appears in *The Methodist Worship Book* as the second collect for the Second Sunday in Ordinary Time.)

First Sunday in Lent

First Collect

Cranmer's collect for this Sunday is the basis for this prayer, although it was much improved by the Joint Liturgical Group in 1968 and 1978, drawing on Colquhoun's *Parish Prayers* (1964). The improvements include the addition of references to Hebrews 4.15 and 7.25 and the disappearance of Cranmer's 'godly motions'.

Second Collect

The two principal inspirations for this collect, from the Canadian book *The Book of Alternative Services* (1985), seem likely to have been John 6.33–59 and the last section of the Prayer of Humble Access.

SECOND SUNDAY IN LENT

First Collect

C.L. MacDonnell wrote the original version of this collect, which was included in *Celebrating Common Prayer* (1992). It echoes Philippians 2.6–8 and Hebrews 5.8.

Second Collect

The original source of this collect is the Gelasian Sacramentary. Cranmer made use of it in 1549 and it appeared in subsequent editions of *The Book of Common Prayer*.

THIRD SUNDAY IN LENT

First Collect

William Reed Huntington wrote this collect in 1882 and it was included in the American *Book of Common Prayer* in 1928 and 1979. Since its appearance in the 1968 and 1978 publications of the Joint Liturgical Group it has been published in most British service books.

Second Collect

This collect, which *The Book of Common Prayer* associates with the previous Sunday, is based on an ancient prayer from the Gelasian Sacramentary and the Sarum Missal.

FOURTH SUNDAY IN LENT

First Collect

Isaiah 50.6 underlies this relatively modern collect, which first appeared in the American *Book of Common Prayer* in 1928. It was included in *The Daily Office* (1968) and *The Daily Office Revised* (1978) of the Joint Liturgical Group, and subsequently in many British service books.

Second Collect

The source of this prayer is the International Commission on English in the Liturgy, whose proposals for the revision of the Roman Sacramentary include it. It is not written strictly in traditional collect form, but it contains many biblical allusions including John 3.16, John 12.32, Ephesians 2.1 and Colossians 3.1.

MOTHERING SUNDAY

Only one collect is provided for this occasion. It is a much-abbreviated version of a prayer written by the liturgist Michael Perham and published in *Enriching the Christian Year* (1993).

FIFTH SUNDAY IN LENT (FIRST SUNDAY OF THE PASSION)

First Collect

This is a fairly modern collect, which first appeared in the *Scottish Prayer Book* of 1929 and was included in *The Daily Office* (1968) and *The Daily Office Revised* (1978) of the Joint Liturgical Group, as well as in *The Methodist Service Book* (1975) and *The Alternative Service Book* (1980).

Second Collect

The second collect is attributed to the *Book of Common Order* (1994), where it indeed appears, but it was first published in Canada, in *The Book of Alternative Services* (1985).

SIXTH SUNDAY IN LENT (SECOND SUNDAY OF THE PASSION OR PALM SUNDAY)

First Collect

This is a simplified version of Cranmer's 1549 collect, which was based on a prayer that had appeared in the Gelasian and Gregorian Sacramentaries and in the Sarum Missal. It looks forward to Good Friday and Easter Day, but makes no reference to the events associated with Palm Sunday. This is in keeping with the long-established tradition that the principal focus of this day is on the approaching Passion and that the Entry into Jerusalem is a subsidiary 'theme'. There are echoes in this collect of Philippians 2.5–11.

Second Collect

In the second collect, from the Scottish *Book of Common Order* (1994), petition is made for a spiritually fruitful observance of Holy Week and Easter. The collect is a modification of a prayer from *The Book of Alternative Services* (1985) and the address, 'God of all-redeeming grace', is a further emendation, made to the Scottish text by the Liturgical Sub-Committee: it is a line from a Charles Wesley hymn (*Hymns & Psalms* 727).

MAUNDY THURSDAY

First Collect

Three collects are provided for this day, which (as we noted on pp. 106ff. above) has multiple associations. The first prayer, which relates to the Lord's Supper, is a shortened version of a collect newly composed for *Lent, Holy Week, Easter* (1984, 1986).

Second Collect

The second collect is also related to the Lord's Supper. Although its immediate source is *The Alternative Service Book* (1980), its origins lie in a medieval collect for the feast of Corpus Christi, which has been attributed to St Thomas Aquinas (1225–74).

Third Collect

It seemed appropriate to the Liturgical Sub-Committee to include a collect which makes reference to Jesus washing his disciples' feet in the Upper Room. The selected collect was originally composed by the Joint Liturgical Group for the Eleventh Sunday after Pentecost and made no reference to the foot-washing. It was used in *The Methodist Service Book* both for the Sunday for which it was written and for Maundy Thursday and it appears in *The Methodist Worship Book* as the first collect for the Twenty-ninth Sunday in Ordinary Time. The revised version of the collect as now printed for Maundy Thursday comes from *A New Zealand Prayer Book* (1989).

GOOD FRIDAY

First Collect

The first of the Good Friday collects comes to us from the Gregorian Sacramentary, via the Sarum Missal and *The Book of Common Prayer*. It has also been associated with the Wednesday of Holy Week.

Second Collect

The second collect has been taken from the *Book of Common Order* (1994) of the Church of Scotland.

Third Collect

This is the Joint Liturgical Group's 1978 revision of another traditional Good Friday collect, which can be traced back to the Gelasian Sacramentary. A metrical version of this prayer appears in *Hymns & Psalms* (547).

Fourth Collect

The fourth collect was written by the Liturgical Sub-Committee for inclusion in the Good Friday service (p. 261). Its tone is very different from Cranmer's Good Friday collect for 'all Jews, Turks, Infidels, and Hereticks', that God will 'take from them all ignorance, hardness of heart, and contempt of [his] Word'. Yet in the prayer that God will 'set us free from prejudice, blindness, and hardness of heart' there is a deliberate echo of Cranmer, and the phrase 'all who look to Abraham as the father of faith' clearly encompasses Jews and Muslims as well as Christians.

HOLY SATURDAY

The collect for Holy Saturday made its first appearance in the Scottish Prayer Book of 1637, before being incorporated into *The Book of Common Prayer* (1662). The version printed in *The Methodist Worship Book* follows the revision of the collect made for *The Alternative Service Book* (1980), except that 'through the merits of him who died . . .' has been substituted for 'through his merits, who died . . .'

EASTER DAY (SERVICES AFTER SUNSET UNTIL EASTER DAWN)

First Collect

This fine collect from New Zealand begins with a sentence which employs the image of light; it is reminiscent of the opening words of the first collect for Christmas Day (Midnight). The prayer then addresses the themes of Baptism and the crossing of the Red Sea, which are associated with the Easter Vigil service.

Second Collect

The second collect comes from the *Book of Common Order* (1994) of the Church of Scotland. It is a revision of a prayer from *The Book of Alternative Services* (1985). As in the first collect, the opening words make much of the metaphor of light, but this prayer develops quite differently from the other, into a prayer that 'we may shine as lights in the world'.

EASTER DAY (SERVICES AFTER DAWN)

First Collect

The earliest known source of this collect is the Gregorian Sacramentary. No version of it appeared in *The Book of Common Prayer* (1662) but it was included in the 1928 proposals for the revision of that book. The version printed in *The Methodist Worship Book* is the work of the Joint Liturgical Group, though 'in the unity of the Holy Spirit' has been substituted for 'and the Holy Spirit'.

Second Collect

The second collect comes from *A New Zealand Service Book* (1989), but it employs some images and phrases from earlier prayers, such as the very Pauline petition that we may be raised 'from the death of sin to the life of righteousness', which appeared in the collect for the Third Sunday after Easter in *The Methodist Service Book* and can be traced back to Thomas Cranmer (1549).

SECOND SUNDAY OF EASTER

First Collect

Since John 20.19–31 is the Gospel lection for this Sunday in all three years, this collect about faith and doubt is very appropriate. It comes from the Canadian publication *The Book of Alternative Services* (1985).

Second Collect

The Emmaus story (Luke 24.13–35) is the set lection for a second service on this Sunday in Year C, though there is no reason why this collect from the International Commission on English in the Liturgy should not be used in other years, particularly appropriate though it is when the Emmaus story is read. Although this is not indicated on p. 541, the Liturgical Sub-Committee has made several alterations to the collect.

THIRD SUNDAY OF EASTER

First Collect

Another collect which is inspired by Luke 24.13–35, this one from the Anglican Church in Canada (1985) emphasizes the recognition of Christ in the breaking of the bread, whereas the second collect for the previous Sunday is concerned with the understanding of the Scriptures.

Second Collect

Janet Morley's *All Desires Known* (1992) is the source of this collect, the use of which is especially appropriate in Year C, when the story of Peter's restoration forms part of the appointed Gospel.

FOURTH SUNDAY OF EASTER

First Collect

Though many collects draw heavily upon Scripture, this prayer is unusual in that, apart from its ending, it is all a quotation from the Bible. The source is Hebrews 13.20f. The use of these verses as a blessing will be familiar to those who remember the first service of Holy Communion from *The Book of Offices* (1936), but their use as a collect seems to date only from 1978 when they appeared in the Joint Liturgical Group's *The Daily Office Revised*.

Second Collect

Like the first collect, the second is a 'Good Shepherd' prayer. It is
'borrowed' from *A New Zealand Prayer Book* (1989). Readings
from John 10, where this imagery originates, occur in each of the
three Lectionary years.

FIFTH SUNDAY OF EASTER

First Collect

The Joint Liturgical Group's *The Daily Office Revised* (1978) is
the source of this collect, based on John 14.6, which is part of the
Gospel lection on this Sunday in Year A. The prayer appeared in
The Methodist Service Book (1975) and *The Alternative Service
Book* (1980) as the collect for the Ninth Sunday before Easter,
when the given 'theme' was 'Christ the Teacher'.

Second Collect

This collect, inspired by Romans 8.38f., is from *A New Zealand
Prayer Book* (1989).

SIXTH SUNDAY OF EASTER

First Collect

The Liturgical Sub-Committee composed this collect, which
alludes to John 6.

Second Collect

By contrast, the second collect is ancient. In its present form, it is
the text published by the Joint Liturgical Group in 1978, but it
dates back to the Leonine Sacramentary and appeared subsequently in the Gregorian Sacramentary, the Sarum Missal, and
successive versions of *The Book of Common Prayer*.

ASCENSION DAY

First Collect

This collect, found in the Gregorian Sacramentary, the Sarum Missal, and various versions of *The Book of Common Prayer*, appears in *The Methodist Worship Book* in a revised version of the Joint Liturgical Group's text of 1978. Cranmer in 1549 substituted 'our Lord' for the words 'our Redeemer' (*redemptorem nostrum*) in the Sarum text. Most subsequent versions of the prayer have followed Cranmer in this, but by printing 'our Saviour' *The Methodist Worship Book* more closely approaches the meaning of the pre-Cranmerian text.

Second Collect

This collect is from *Uniting in Worship* (1988). It not only celebrates the Ascension, but looks forward to Pentecost and alludes to the Great Commission of Matthew 28.18ff.

SEVENTH SUNDAY OF EASTER (SUNDAY IN ASCENSIONTIDE)

First Collect

The Franciscan prayer book *Celebrating Common Prayer* (1992) is the source of this collect, which is clearly inspired by Psalm 24.

Second Collect

This collect from New Zealand (1979) is, like the second collect for Ascension Day, inspired by the closing verses of Matthew 28.

PENTECOST

First Collect

This traditional collect for Pentecost, found in the Gregorian Sacramentary, the Sarum Missal, the 1549 version and subsequent versions of *The Book of Common Prayer* and many other books, emphasizes the teaching and strengthening work of the Holy Spirit.

Second Collect

The second collect was written by the Joint Liturgical Group in time to be included in *The Methodist Service Book* (1975), prior to its publication in *The Daily Office Revised* (1978). It draws heavily on Acts 2.1–4, and concentrates on the inspirational and empowering roles of the Holy Spirit, upon which the Church's mission depends.

Third Collect

The Canadian prayer book *The Book of Alternative Services* (1985) is the source of this collect, which differs from the other two by explicitly linking Pentecost and Easter.

TRINITY SUNDAY

First Collect

The first collect dates from the Gregorian Sacramentary, and is thus older than the observance of Trinity Sunday, which began only in the tenth century. The prayer found its way into the Sarum Missal and the various editions of *The Book of Common Prayer*.

Second Collect

The second collect was written by the Liturgical Sub-Committee.

EIGHTH SUNDAY IN ORDINARY TIME

The collects for this Sunday have been discussed on p. 199 above.

NINTH SUNDAY IN ORDINARY TIME

First Collect

The first collect was written by Thomas Cranmer for *The Book of Common Prayer* (1549). It is based on Ephesians 2.19–22.

Second Collect

The second collect is the work of the Liturgical Sub-Committee, based on Lamentations 3.23.

TENTH SUNDAY IN ORDINARY TIME

First Collect

The Liturgical Sub-Committee composed the first collect with the Lectionary readings for Year A in mind.

Second Collect

This prayer comes from the South African source *Modern Collects* (1972), whence it found its way into *The Methodist Service Book* (1975) and *The Daily Office Revised* (1978).

ELEVENTH SUNDAY IN ORDINARY TIME

First Collect

This collect was written by the Liturgical Sub-Committee. Its opening lines echo Habakkuk 3.3 and Psalm 19.1–4.

Second Collect

This prayer is a composition by the International Commission on English in the Liturgy. The Liturgical Sub-Committee inserted the reference to 'extravagant love' (in place of 'immeasurable love'); this makes the collect especially suitable for Year C, when Luke 7.36—8.3 is the appointed Gospel.

TWELFTH SUNDAY IN ORDINARY TIME

First Collect

Two recently written collects are provided for this Sunday. The
first, by the International Commission on English in the Liturgy,
was written for this Sunday. It is full of biblical allusions, including Genesis 1.1–2, Galatians 4.4 and Revelation 21.5.

Second Collect

Although the basis of the second collect is a prayer from
Celebrating Common Prayer (1992), the first two lines were substituted for the original words by the Liturgical Sub-Committee.
The address is a quotation from a Charles Wesley hymn (*Hymns
& Psalms* 726) and the second line ('you call your Church to love
and praise') is an allusion to the Methodist Conference
Statement on the Nature of the Church, entitled *Called to Love
and Praise*, which was published in draft form in 1995 and
adopted in its final form by the Conference of 1999.

THIRTEENTH SUNDAY IN ORDINARY TIME

First Collect

This collect, based on Galatians 5.22, is substantially the work of
the Joint Liturgical Group. In a slightly different form it was
included in *The Methodist Service Book* (1975) and *The Alternative Service Book* (1980).

Second Collect

Some of the phrases of this prayer, written by the Liturgical Sub-
Committee, call to mind Romans 6.12–23 and Psalm 130, which
are appointed for Years A and B respectively.

FOURTEENTH SUNDAY IN ORDINARY TIME

First Collect

The source of this collect is *A New Zealand Prayer Book* (1989). The opening words, 'Servant Lord', are suggestive of John 13.14.

Second Collect

The second collect was composed for this Sunday by the International Commission on English in the Liturgy. It links worship, spirituality and mission in a helpful way.

FIFTEENTH SUNDAY IN ORDINARY TIME

First Collect

Both collects for this day come from *A New Zealand Prayer Book* (1989). The address in the first, 'gentle God', is unusual; it is one of many examples of the way in which the collects in *The Methodist Worship Book* employ a wider range of words and images in addressing God than has traditionally been the custom.

Second Collect

This prayer, though a model of traditional collect structure, combines the themes of unity, justice and peace in a way that makes it a thoroughly modern prayer. The collect also appears, either by accident or by design, as the first collect for the Thirtieth Sunday in Ordinary Time.

SIXTEENTH SUNDAY IN ORDINARY TIME

First Collect

The Methodist Worship Book correctly attributes this prayer to *Uniting in Worship* (1988). Underlying it, however, are several earlier sources, including Matthew 6.25–34, Colossians 3.1–2, and the second collect for the Nineteenth Sunday in Ordinary Time, which, as will be indicated below, has a long history.

Second Collect

This composition by the International Commission on English in the Liturgy is concerned with alertness to God in everyday living. It has resonances of the Emmaus story (Luke 24.13–35).

SEVENTEENTH SUNDAY IN ORDINARY TIME

First Collect

Though *The Methodist Worship Book* attributes the first collect to *The Book of Alternative Services* (1985), with alterations, it appeared ten years before that book was published, in *The Methodist Service Book* (1975). It was a composition of the Joint Liturgical Group, though by the time that the Group's *The Daily Office Revised* (1978) appeared, it had been significantly amended. As a case study of the way in which the editors of liturgical publications rewrite and revise texts, a number of variants of this prayer are set out in the table opposite:

Among the many interesting points suggested by the five versions of the collect which are printed in the table, is the identification, in the three most recent, of 'the true and living bread' with 'Jesus Christ our Lord'. This very properly reflects John 6.51, and John 6 is, of course, the primary inspiration of the prayer.

Second Collect

The second collect was written by the Joint Liturgical Group and used in *The Methodist Service Book* (1975) and *The Alternative Service Book* (1980) for the Fourth Sunday after Pentecost, Year 1, when the Lectionary 'theme' was given as 'The Freedom of the Sons of God'. The collect is based on Galatians 3.26—4.7, which was the 'controlling lesson' (see below, p. 225) for that Sunday.

The Methodist Service Book (1975)	*The Daily Office Revised* (1978)	*The Book of Alternative Services* (1985)	*The Methodist Worship Book* (1999)	*Common Worship* (2000)
Almighty God, whose Son Jesus Christ fed the hungry with the bread of the Kingdom and the word of his mouth; renew your people with your heavenly grace; and in all our weakness sustain us by your true and living bread; through Jesus Christ our Lord.	Almighty God, who revealed in signs and miracles the wonder of your saving love: renew your people with your heavenly grace, and in all our weakness sustain us by your mighty power; through Jesus Christ our Lord.	Almighty God, your Son Jesus Christ fed the hungry with the bread of his life and the word of his kingdom. Renew your people with your heavenly grace, and in all our weakness sustain us by your true and living bread, who lives and reigns with you and the Holy Spirit, one God, now and for ever.	Gracious God, your Son Jesus Christ fed the hungry with the bread of life and the word of your kingdom. Renew your people with your heavenly grace, and in all our weakness sustain us by your true and living bread, even Jesus Christ our Lord.	God of all grace, your Son Jesus Christ fed the hungry with the bread of his life and the word of his kingdom: renew your people with your heavenly grace; and in all our weakness sustain us by your true and living bread; who is alive and reigns, now and for ever.

EIGHTEENTH SUNDAY IN ORDINARY TIME

First Collect

Although the original version of this collect, which is strongly influenced by John 6.27, 35, 41, is the work of the International Commission on English in the Liturgy, the Liturgical Sub-Committee has rewritten it to a considerable extent.

Second Collect

This composition by the Joint Liturgical Group appeared in *The Methodist Service Book* (1975) and in *The Alternative Service Book* (1980). It has clearly been inspired by John 4.24 and Hebrews 10.20–23.

NINETEENTH SUNDAY IN ORDINARY TIME

First Collect

Uniting in Worship (1988) provides yet another collect which reflects verses from John 6.

Second Collect

Loosely based on 1 Corinthians 4.14, 18, this collect can be traced back through successive editions of *The Book of Common Prayer* to the Sarum Missal and the Gregorian Sacramentary.

TWENTIETH SUNDAY IN ORDINARY TIME

First Collect

The International Commission on English in the Liturgy supplies both the collects for this Sunday. Both contain biblical allusions. In the first, the influence of Luke 14.12–24, Ephesians 2.19, Exodus 16.12 and Psalm 51.12 can be detected. 'Satisfy the hunger of those gathered in this house of prayer' was amended by the Liturgical Sub-Committee to 'hear the cries of the hungry', an emendation which significantly alters the thrust of the collect.

Second Collect

In this collect, allusions to Luke 12.49, Philippians 2.8, Mark 10.38 and Hebrews 12.1–2 are blended into a prayer for faithful endurance.

TWENTY-FIRST SUNDAY IN ORDINARY TIME

First Collect

This short collect was written by the Liturgical Sub-Committee. In its allusions to the Exodus, it expresses the conviction that a concern for justice and freedom for all people is in accordance with God's will.

Second Collect

Unity and witness are the twin themes of this collect, which, though it appears in the *Book of Common Order* (1994) of the Church of Scotland, to which *The Methodist Worship Book* attributes it, was composed for *The Book of Alternative Services* (1985).

TWENTY-SECOND SUNDAY IN ORDINARY TIME

First Collect

The Exodus story also underlies this collect, which, though taken by *The Methodist Worship Book* from *A New Zealand Prayer Book* (1989), is based on a collect written by the Joint Liturgical Group, which was itself inspired by a prayer in *The Book of Common Worship of the Church of South India* (1963).

Second Collect

The source of the second collect is *Uniting in Worship* (1988).

Twenty-third Sunday in Ordinary time

First Collect

In composing this new collect, the Liturgical Sub-Committee was clearly influenced by Charles Wesley's hymn 'Captain of Israel's host' (*Hymns & Psalms* 62), inspired by Exodus 13.21.

Second Collect

By contrast, the second collect is ancient, its first known appearance being in the Gregorian Sacramentary. It was translated by Cranmer for *The Book of Common Prayer* (1549). In the 1662 version of the Prayer Book, this prayer was used, not as a Sunday collect, but towards the end of the ordination service.

Twenty-fourth Sunday in Ordinary time

First Collect

The Joint Liturgical Group wrote this collect for use on the Eleventh Sunday after Pentecost, when the stated Lectionary theme was 'The Witnessing Community'. It is based on 2 Corinthians 5.19f.

Second Collect

The source of the second collect, notable for its imaginative use of feminine imagery, is *Uniting in Worship* (1988).

Twenty-fifth Sunday in Ordinary time

First Collect

There are versions of this collect in the Gelasian and Gregorian Sacramentaries, the Sarum Missal, successive editions of *The Book of Common Prayer* and most modern service books. In the Joint Liturgical Group's publications of 1968 and 1978 it was linked to the theme 'Citizens of Heaven'.

Second Collect

The story of God's provision for Israel in the wilderness, and particularly Numbers 11.9, underlies this collect, written by the Liturgical Sub-Committee.

Twenty-sixth Sunday in Ordinary time

First Collect

The *Book of Common Order* (1994) included this collect, amending the original text, which was printed in *The Book of Alternative Services* (1985). The collect is based on John 4.14. In *The Methodist Worship Book*, the words 'turn to' have been substituted for 'thirst for' which appeared in both the Canadian original and the Scottish version.

Second Collect

This is a version of the first collect for the Second Sunday of the Passion (see p. 203 above), prepared by the Joint Liturgical Group, in which that ancient collect's indebtedness to Philippians 2.5–11 is made more obvious.

Twenty-seventh Sunday in Ordinary time

First Collect

Celebrating Common Prayer (1992) supplies this prayer, written by Michael Perham, which reflects several biblical passages, including Psalm 1.1–2, Psalm 119.2, 97 and Romans 8.21.

Second Collect

This collect is little altered from the form in which it appeared in *The Book of Common Prayer* (1662), where it was the collect for the Third Sunday after Epiphany, except that 'stretch out your hand' is substituted for 'stretch forth thy right hand'.

Twenty-eighth Sunday in Ordinary time

First Collect

This is the only collect in *The Methodist Worship Book* which has been taken from *The Divine Office* (1974). There are echoes, some of them faint, of many biblical passages.

Second Collect

Apart from the substitution of 'God' for 'Lord' as the first word, this is the Joint Liturgical Group's version of a collect which, by way of all editions of *The Book of Common Prayer* and the Sarum Missal, can be traced back to the Gelasian and Gregorian Sacramentaries.

Twenty-ninth Sunday in Ordinary time

First Collect

See Maundy Thursday (Third Collect).

Second Collect

Though this prayer is a little indebted to the prayer book of the Church of South India, and, in its preamble, draws on Genesis 1, it is substantially the work of the Joint Liturgical Group (1968, revised 1978).

Thirtieth Sunday in Ordinary time

First Collect

See the Fifteenth Sunday in Ordinary Time (Second Collect).

Second Collect

Uniting in Worship (1988) is the source of this collect.

ALL SAINTS

First Collect

Ephesians 4.11–13 was Thomas Cranmer's inspiration when he wrote this collect in 1549. The attribution to *Celebrating Common Prayer* (1992) is inexplicable. Numerous versions of this prayer exist, none of which is identical to that in *The Methodist Worship Book*, but the book responsible for substituting 'inexpressible' for the 'unspeakable' of Cranmer's original was *The Book of Alternative Services* (1985).

Second Collect

This new collect is the work of the Liturgical Sub-Committee.

THIRTY-FIRST SUNDAY IN ORDINARY TIME

First Collect

Though the basis of this prayer is found in the Leonine Sacramentary, it was the Joint Liturgical Group's rediscovery of it that made possible its inclusion in *The Methodist Service Book* (1975), *The Alternative Service Book* (1980), and many more recent service books. The collect is strongly influenced by Mark 12.29–31 and Romans 13.10.

Second Collect

The biblical passages which come together in this collect, from the International Commission on English in the Liturgy, are Isaiah 49.15 and Matthew 6.31–34. The address, 'All-embracing God', was substituted by the Liturgical Sub-Committee for 'Lord God'.

THIRTY-SECOND SUNDAY IN ORDINARY TIME

First Collect

The original text of this splendid collect, with its allusion to 1 John 4.18, was written by Sid Hedges. The prayer was then printed in an altered form in *Celebrating Common Prayer* (1992); further slight amendments were made for *The Methodist Worship Book*, where the collect is also given for Remembrance Sunday.

Second Collect

The Joint Liturgical Group used phrases from a prayer in the Roman Missal when composing this collect for *The Daily Office* (1968). It appeared in *The Methodist Service Book* (1975) and *The Alternative Service Book* (1980).

THIRTY-THIRD SUNDAY IN ORDINARY TIME

First Collect

The author of the original version of this collect was Francis Paget, Bishop of Oxford (1902–11). It was included in the proposed revision of *The Book of Common Prayer* in 1928 and in *The Alternative Service Book* (1980).

Second Collect

The Book of Alternative Services (1985) is the source of this collect, which also appears in the *Book of Common Order* (1994) of the Church of Scotland.

THE SUNDAY BEFORE ADVENT

First Collect

The South African publication *Modern Collects* (1972) was the original source of this prayer, which then appeared in *The*

Methodist Service Book (1975), *The Daily Office Revised* (1978), and *The Alternative Service Book* (1980). The collect is also set for this Sunday in *Common Worship* (2000).

Second Collect

The famous 'Stir up . . .' collect dates from the Gregorian Sacramentary, was used by Thomas Cranmer in 1549, and has appeared in subsequent versions of *The Book of Common Prayer* and most service books which stand in the Prayer Book tradition.

BIBLE SUNDAY

This is another well-known collect, written by Thomas Cranmer for *The Book of Common Prayer* (1549). It was based on Romans 15.4.

CHRISTIAN UNITY

First Collect

Originally published in 1989 by what is now Churches Together in Britain and Ireland, this collect, 'the Pilgrim Prayer', reflects the phrase, 'not strangers, but pilgrims', which was widely used in an ecumenical context at the time. Its ultimate source is Hebrews 11.13 where, however, the 'strangers' and the 'pilgrims' are one and the same people!

Second Collect

The second collect comes from the *Book of Common Order* (1994) of the Church of Scotland. Like the first, it links unity with mission.

CHURCH ANNIVERSARY

The basis of this collect is a prayer written by the late Raymond George for *Companion to the Lectionary, Volume 3* (1983), edited by the present writer.

HARVEST THANKSGIVING

The first three lines of this collect are the work of the Liturgical Sub-Committee, but the remainder closely follows a collect for the Rogation Days in *The Alternative Service Book* (1980), which itself employs phrases from *The Book of Common Prayer* (1662).

JOHN AND CHARLES WESLEY

First Collect

This is a prayer of the Methodist Sacramental Fellowship, the original version of which dates back to the early days of the Fellowship. Several themes, including evangelism, spirituality, word and sacrament, and unity, are combined within this collect.

Second Collect

This collect is a tribute to the esteem in which the Wesley brothers are held in the wider Church; it comes from the Franciscan publication *Celebrating Common Prayer* (1992), for which it was written by Brother Tristram SSF.

NEW YEAR: WATCHNIGHT

First Collect

The first collect is the work of the Liturgical Sub-Committee. Its preamble contains a reference to Psalm 90.4 (Psalm 90 is one of two Psalms listed in the Lectionary for this occasion) and there is an allusion to Psalm 148.2 in the fourth line.

Second Collect

The second collect comes from the *Book of Common Order* (1994) of the Church of Scotland. Its opening lines take account of the fact that New Year falls during the season of Christmas.

REMEMBRANCE SUNDAY

See the first collect for the Thirty-second Sunday in Ordinary Time.

Our survey of the sources of the collects in *The Methodist Worship Book* should have provided ample justification for the assertion in the Introduction (p. 520) that they are 'treasures old and new'. Some were written as recently as the last decade of the twentieth century; others are as old as the fourth century. Taken together, they are a potent sign of the living tradition of the Christian Church.

The Lectionary

As we have seen, the version of the Calendar which was adopted in *The Methodist Service Book* was that proposed by the Joint Liturgical Group in 1967. This Calendar was associated with a Lectionary on a two-year cycle. For each principal service three readings were suggested: Old Testament, Epistle and Gospel. On any given Sunday, one of these would be the 'controlling lesson', which would determine the 'theme' for the day, and the other two lections were chosen to fit in with that theme.

Although this did much to popularize the use of a Lectionary, a number of criticisms came to be levelled against the Joint Liturgical Group's Lectionary. In the first place, after the two-year cycle had been repeated several times, it was felt that the same passages were recurring too frequently. An associated criticism was that the coverage of Scripture was not adequate; many important passages, it was said, were never read. There was also disapproval of the tendency for preachers to address the stated 'theme' rather than the Scripture passages themselves.

The Joint Liturgical Group responded to these criticisms by producing a new Lectionary, on the basis of a four-year cycle, which was adopted by the Methodist Conference in 1991 and remained in use until it was superseded on Advent Sunday 1998 by the Lectionary which is provided for the Principal Service in *The Methodist Worship Book*. In the four-year Lectionary, each of the four Gospels provided most of the Gospel readings for a year. The other readings continued to be linked in some way to the Gospel, but themes were no longer stated and it was not always easy to detect the connections that had been in the compilers' minds.

The second Joint Liturgical Group Lectionary had many merits, however, and might have been carried forward into *The Methodist Worship Book*, had it not been for the very widespread acceptance of the *Revised Common Lectionary* (1992), produced by the Consultation on Common Texts. Its adoption or likely adoption by most ecumenical partners in Britain and abroad made this Lectionary with its three-year cycle the obvious choice for inclusion in the new service book. It is well described on p. 521, where reference is also made to the provision of a Lectionary for a Second Service. It was clear to the Liturgical Sub-Committee that such a Lectionary was needed, but the *Revised Common Lectionary* supplied readings for only one service. The Sub-Committee did not believe that there was any point in trying to devise its own second Lectionary since the Liturgical Commission of the Church of England had produced one, which was designed to accompany the *Revised Common Lectionary*, and permission was sought and granted for its inclusion in *The Methodist Worship Book*.

Glossary

Absolution: See *Declaration of Forgiveness*.

Advent: The period of time, including four Sundays, with which the Christian year begins. It ends on *Christmas* Eve. Advent is both a period of preparation for *Christmas* and a time for reflection upon the Christian hope of Christ's coming in glory.

Affirmation of Faith: A statement of belief, other than in the form of one of the three *Historic Creeds*.

Antiphon: A verse, often from the Bible, which is said or sung before and/or after, and sometimes during, a Psalm or *canticle*.

Antiphonal reading: A reading in which two groups of people, or the leader and the congregation, speak alternately.

Apocryphal books: Those books which are included in the Greek version of the Old Testament, but not in the Hebrew Bible.

Apostles' Creed: This ancient statement of Christian belief developed from questions and answers asked of candidates for *Baptism* in the early Church.

Ascensiontide: The part of *Easter* which celebrates Christ's ascension into heaven. It begins on Ascension Day and ends ten days later, at *Pentecost*.

Ash Wednesday: The first day of *Lent*.

Baptism: The *sacrament* of initiation instituted by Christ, in which a person is dipped in water or water is poured upon a person in the name of the Father, the Son and the Holy Spirit.

Baptistry: A pool or tank of water used for *Baptism*.

Baptizand: A candidate for *Baptism*.

Bidding: An invitation to prayer on a stated theme or themes.

Blessing: Often called the 'Benediction', the Blessing is that declaration of God's favour which occurs towards the end of an act of worship. The term is also used for words said over people (for example, in Marriage) or objects.

Byzantine liturgy: The ancient form of *liturgy* which has dominated the worship of many of the Orthodox Churches. It is named after Byzantium (later Constantinople) which was the principal centre of the Eastern part of the Roman Empire at the time when distinctively Byzantine liturgy arose.

Calendar: The systematic allocation of the Church's year to seasons such as *Advent*, *Christmas*, *Lent*, *Easter* and to *Ordinary Time*.

Canticle: A sacred song, not in metrical form, but Psalm-like in structure. Many canticles, but not all, consist of verses from the Bible.

Christmas: A period of 12 days, starting with Christmas Day, during which the birth of Jesus Christ is celebrated.

Collect: A short prayer with a distinctive structure (outlined on p. 520 of *The Methodist Worship Book*), often assigned to a particular Sunday or occasion or to a specific service.

Committal: The part of the funeral *liturgy* during which the body of a person who has died is committed to the earth or to be cremated.

Communicant: A person who receives and consumes bread and wine at a service of *Holy Communion*.

Communion: According to context, this term is either a synonym for *Holy Communion* or refers to a branch of the Christian Church (as in 'The Reception of Christians of Other Communions . . .').

Conference: See *Methodist Conference*.

Confirmation: The service which includes prayer with the *laying on of hands* which follows *Baptism*, either immediately or on a subsequent occasion. Its meaning is discussed in Chapter Seven.

Connexion: In Methodist usage, this word refers to the whole of the British Methodist Church.

Connexional: Pertaining to the *Connexion*.

Consultation on Common Texts: An ecumenical body, mainly, though not exclusively, representative of churches in North America. The Consultation prepared *The Revised Common Lectionary* which is used for the Principal Service in *The Methodist Worship Book*'s Lectionary.

Creed: See *Historic Creeds*.

Deacon: A person ordained to a ministry of service, distinct from, though equal in status to, *presbyteral* ministry.

Declaration of Forgiveness: A statement, made after a prayer of confession, usually by the person presiding at a service, to the effect that God forgives the sins of those who are penitent. In some traditions this is known as 'Absolution'.

Deed of Union: Part of the written constitution of the Methodist Church. See also *Standing Orders*.

Diaconal: Pertaining to a *deacon*.

Easter: A period of 50 days, extending from Easter Day to *Pentecost*. Up to the fortieth day, which is Ascension Day, the season is a celebration of Christ's resurrection. *Ascensiontide* begins on Ascension Day.

Elements: The bread and wine used at *Holy Communion*.

English Language Liturgical Consultation: A body established in 1985 with representatives of ecumenical liturgical groups, including the *Joint Liturgical Group*, from many parts of the English-speaking world.

Epiclesis: An invocation of the Holy Spirit, or a request to God to send the Holy Spirit. An *epiclesis* is an integral part of a *Eucharistic Prayer*.

Epiphany: A festival day (6 January) which commemorates the visit of the Magi (Matthew 2) and, in some traditions, the Baptism of Christ. The word means 'manifestation'.

Epistle: According to context, either one of the New Testament letters, for example, Colossians or James, or a reading from the New Testament, other than a *Gospel*. The latter use of the term embraces *lections* from the Acts of the Apostles, from the New Testament letters and from Revelation.

Eucharist: A term widely used in many branches of the Church as a title for the *Lord's Supper*. Derived from a Greek word which means 'thanksgiving', the term emphasizes the joyful celebration which is central to this *sacrament*.

Eucharistic: Pertaining to the *Eucharist*.

Eucharistic Prayer: See *Great Prayer of Thanksgiving.*

Font: A vessel used to hold water for *Baptism.* Fonts may be free-standing, though some churches use smaller fonts which are placed on a table.

Gospel: This word is used in two different ways. According to context, it means either the Good News of the Christian faith, or a reading from one of the four New Testament Gospels.

Great Prayer of Thanksgiving: Also known as the *Eucharistic Prayer*, this is the central prayer of the *Eucharist.* Its constituent parts are discussed in Chapter Eight.

Greeting: An exchange of sentences between the person presiding at a service and the congregation, for example, 'The Lord be with you. **And also with you.**'

Hand of Fellowship: This action, once known as the 'right hand of fellowship', is included in services of admission, commissioning, welcome, and reception into membership. It is a handshake in a *liturgical* context.

Historic Creeds: There are three 'Historic Creeds', of which two, the *Apostles' Creed* and the *Nicene Creed*, are used in *The Methodist Worship Book*. The third, the Athanasian Creed, is not included.

Holy Communion: The *sacrament* of the *Lord's Supper.*

Holy Saturday: The last day of *Holy Week* and the day before *Easter* Day.

Holy Week: The final week of *Lent* and the second of *Passiontide.*

Initiation Services: The services – *Baptism* and *Confirmation* – during which people are initiated into the Christian Community.

International Commission on English in the Liturgy: An agency of 26 Roman Catholic national or international conferences of bishops.

Johannine: Pertaining to the *Gospel* according to St John.

Joint Liturgical Group: An ecumenical body, with representatives from the major churches of England, Scotland and Wales, whose many influential publications include *The Calendar and Lectionary* (1967), *The Daily Office* (1968) and *The Daily Office Revised* (1978).

Kontakion: This term, which comes from the Orthodox tradition, now refers to a short hymn which is read or sung during the *Eucharist* and certain *offices*. At an earlier period, the *kontakion* was appreciably longer.

Law, reading from the: A *lection* from the Old Testament books Genesis, Exodus, Leviticus, Numbers, or Deuteronomy.

Laying on of hands: An action performed in conjunction with prayer for one of a number of purposes, including *Confirmation*, *Ordination* and healing. See above, pp. 70f.

Lection: A passage of Scripture, prescribed in a *Lectionary*.

Lectionary: Either a systematic scheme of Bible readings for Sundays and other days in the *Calendar* or, in some traditions, a book containing the full text of those readings.

Lent: A period which extends from *Ash Wednesday* to *Holy Saturday* and which is a time for penitence and self-examination. It includes *Passiontide*.

Litany: A prayer, usually of intercession, made up of variable V*ersicles* and variable or invariable *Responses*.

Liturgical: Pertaining to *liturgy*. The word is sometimes used, rather loosely, to distinguish 'formal' or 'liturgical' acts of worship, as printed in a service book, from 'free' services.

Liturgiologist: A student of *liturgy*.

Liturgist: A writer or editor of services, or a *liturgiologist*.

Liturgy: There are several ways in which this word is employed. In this book, 'liturgy' is used as a synonym for worship and 'a liturgy' means a form of service.

Lord's Supper: The *sacrament* instituted by Christ in which bread and wine are consumed in remembrance of him. See also *Holy Communion* and *Eucharist*.

Markan: Pertaining to the *Gospel* according to St Mark.

Matthean: Pertaining to the *Gospel* according to St Matthew.

Methodist Conference: The Conference is the supreme governing body of British Methodism, and exercises oversight over the life of the whole Methodist Church.

Nicene Creed: This *Historic Creed* takes its name from the Council of Nicaea (AD 325), though in its present form it dates from the Council of Constantinople (AD 381). If a statement of faith is to be included in the *Eucharist*, it is usually the Nicene Creed.

Office: A short service of prayer and praise for use at a particular time of day (such as 'Prayer in the Morning') or on a specific occasion (such as 'An Office of Commendation'). The word is derived from the Latin word *officium*, which means 'duty'.

Ordinand: A candidate for *Ordination*.

Ordinary Time (Ordinary Seasons): Those parts of the *Calendar* which fall between the Sunday after *Epiphany* and *Shrove Tuesday* inclusive or between the Monday after the Day of *Pentecost* and the day before the First Sunday of *Advent* inclusive.

Ordination: The setting apart of a person, by prayer and the *laying on of hands*, for *diaconal* or *presbyteral* ministry.

Passiontide: The last two weeks of *Lent*, the second of which is *Holy Week*.

Pentecost: The fiftieth and final day of the *Easter* season and the day which commemorates the gift of the Holy Spirit to the apostles, as recorded in Acts 2.

Preamble: That part of a *collect* which follows the opening address to God and refers to a characteristic of God's nature.

Presbyter: A person ordained to the ministry of the Word and Sacraments.

Presbyteral: Pertaining to a *presbyter*.

Presiding minister: In Methodist usage, the term 'presiding minister' means a *presbyter* or person with an authorization from the *Conference* to preside at the *Lord's Supper*. What this means in practice is spelled out in Note 2 on p. 115 of *The Methodist Worship Book*.

Probationer: A person who is stationed in a *presbyteral* or *diaconal* appointment, but who has not yet been ordained as a *presbyter* or *deacon*.

Prophets, reading from the: A *lection* from an Old Testament book which records the message of a prophet, for example, Isaiah or Amos.

Responses: See *Versicles and Responses*.

Sacrament: In Methodist usage, there are two sacraments: *Baptism* and the *Lord's Supper*, which were instituted by Christ himself and which are of 'perpetual obligation' for the Church. In the sacraments, material things (water, bread and wine) are both the symbols of God's grace and the means through which it is bestowed.

Sentences: Words, usually from the Bible, spoken at the start of an act of worship and sometimes during it.

Shrove Tuesday: The day before *Ash Wednesday* and thus the last day of the period of *Ordinary Time* that precedes *Lent*.

Standing Orders: The Standing Orders of the Methodist Church are part of that Church's constitution. They consist of rules, made by the *Methodist Conference*, which, alongside other provisions, such as the *Deed of Union*, govern the Church's life.

Synoptic: A term applied to the Gospels according to Matthew, Mark and Luke, and derived from the Greek for 'sharing a common point of view'.

Trinitarian: Pertaining to the Holy Trinity – God the Father, God the Son, and God the Holy Spirit.

Versicles and Responses: These terms are used for sentences in prayers, said responsively by the leader and the people respectively. A well-known example is the versicle 'Lord, in your mercy', to which the response is '**hear our prayer**'.

Vigil: A service, usually involving prayer and quiet meditation, held on the evening preceding a festival or other holy day, or, in some traditions, before a funeral.

Wisdom Literature: Certain parts of the Old Testament – Proverbs, Job and Ecclesiastes – and some *Apocryphal books*.

Index